cooking
with
love

KEITH SQUIRES

cooking with love

DRU PUBLICATIONS

Contents

Introduction

*F*or the past 30 years I have been involved in overseeing and creating the culinary delights at the Dru Yoga and Wellbeing centres in the UK and abroad. I realised years ago how vital a part food plays in the experience people have—for some folks it even seems to be the main thing!

Many people ask me how we prepare the food.
'What are the secrets behind your cooking, Keith?'
My personal secret is that the way you cook the food,
as well as the ingredients and the method, makes a huge
difference to how it turns out.

So here are some of my recipes and the knowledge applied.
I hope they will help you love cooking more with each day.

Our main residential centre is in Snowdonia National Park in North Wales, set in a glacial valley dominated by the ancient Cambrian Mountains. Clear mountain streams run off the hills into the valley, rivers and waterfalls below.

Each week people from all over the world pass through our doors to enjoy our retreats and courses and to participate in our volunteer programmes. The delicious wholesome food combines with the inspiring location, relaxations and therapies to give an experience that fully satisfies the senses.

Guests often want to take our chefs home with them so they can continue to have Dru food at home. Obviously we can't let you do that but this book is the next best thing—your guide to creating a Dru kitchen in your own home.

Gwely a brecwast
B&B
Snowdonia
Mountain Lodge
Ensuite accommodation
dru
International
Training Centre
Canolfan Hyfforddi Ryngwladol
Education for health and wellbeing

Dru Yoga is part of the Ayurvedic system of health. I've therefore included an introduction to Ayurveda, with tips and recipes, to help you understand about your own body's constitution. Ayurveda recommends a mainly vegetarian diet. To help with that, there's a chapter on the different aspects of healthy vegetarian eating.

In this book the most important message is all in the title, 'Cooking with Love'. Here I reveal everything you need to know about how to add that extra something to make your food unique and special. You'll also learn fascinating facts about the nutrition, history, mythology and legends of my favourite ingredients.

My childhood headmaster used to say, 'I've taught them everything I know and still they know nothing.'

I'm sure that won't be the case after you've read this book. There's something here for everyone, even if I say it myself!

Me aged 9
watering my
vegetable
garden

Early
Beginnings...

I discovered cooking at the age of 9, making cakes and bread at home from my mother's recipe books. Luckily Mum was very encouraging and Dad good naturedly ate everything I proffered.

Once I got going I soon needed a new outlet—my father's appetite couldn't keep up! So I began to take my culinary creations to school. My friends loved them and I found a new popularity. It's when I first discovered that sharing food creates friendship and brings people together.

It was a small village school, with twenty boys in our class. The headmaster, Mr Woodruff, was a stern but fatherly man. He loved my cakes and even remarked privately that they were better than his wife's baking.

Soon my friends started baking too, and it actually became a bit competitive—we vied with each other to see who could make the best bread and lightest cakes. Instead of running around like normal boys, we spent the break times eating and sharing our baked goodies and eagerly presenting them to the headmaster. As a result we all started to put on weight, and our class can clearly be identified on the old school photos as being slightly more rotund and contented looking than the older and younger boys.

Our interest in food then went beyond cooking to gardening and growing herbs. Our headmaster allowed us to cultivate parts of the school grounds and we each developed our own vegetable patch. We set up a shed complete with a gas stove to make tea. Men love their sheds, but we started early; we were like old men in the bodies of ten year old boys. We spent our spare time discussing seeds and gardening tools, followed by a daily inspection of each other's gardens. Our delighted headmaster held us up as splendid examples of how young men should be. Needless to say, we basked in the glory and pretended to look down on the rest of the boys who spent their time in more childish pursuits such as running around.

Mr Woodruff was so pleased with our class that he took us on a fantastic summer trip to Switzerland by Lake Lugano. We couldn't go by jet plane back then, so it was a classic boys' adventure—by land and sea. We took the ferry from Dover to Calais, followed by a 24-hour train journey through France to the Italian-speaking part of Switzerland.

My classmates
who caught
the cooking
bug from me!

We loved the continental food, boat trips, taking the cable car to the top of the mountain and walking down again through cool green forests. Mr Woodruff was a true British gentleman, complete with an air of confident superiority (especially in France, we noticed). He could speak French and Italian, and made sure that 'his boys' got the best of everything.

I nearly pushed my luck.

Mr Woodruff was a chain smoker and one day, as he was lighting a cigarette, I said, 'You shouldn't smoke, Sir.' Sudden silence (like in a spaghetti western when the outlaw walks into a bar and the piano stops playing). Everyone froze. In those days you never, ever corrected a teacher.

'And why not, young Squires?' Mr Woodruff asked quietly. 'Because my Grandad died a few months ago from smoking,' I replied in sweaty earnest. He smiled suddenly, much to everyone's astonishment and my relief. From then on, every time he lit a cigarette I would always say to him, 'You shouldn't smoke, Sir.' He would nod sagely but carry on anyway. I was the only boy afforded this special privilege. Anyone else who tried it got a clip round the ear. And so began my career in health advice.

A couple of years later I joined the Boy Scouts and was instantly dwarfed by 15 year olds twice my size. With no proper scoutmaster the big boys ran it their way—gangland style. I found a survival strategy. As luck would have it my Dad owned a large builders merchants and every day he'd come home and empty out his pockets on the kitchen counter. This just happened to be at my eye level and I soon found I could harvest off a few coins without being noticed. I used this money to buy bags of chips for the bullies during the break. I suddenly became really popular, discovering that free food was the best way to distract the bullies! I found I loved taking the orders, running up to the chip shop and rushing back to dish them out. It started getting really expensive though. Luckily, I was soon old enough to start working for pocket money in my Dad's shop—so I then had a legitimate source of income.

After school I moved to Bangor to study at the university—it was there that I met the Dru team. I used to help out at their fruit and vegetable shop (now a health store called Dimensions). Late one morning I felt really hungry. It didn't seem right to go upstairs to make food just for myself, so I cooked enough food for everyone. That decision changed my life. The next day everyone asked me to be the resident chef. I'd created a new role for myself! It was mostly trial and error to begin with. The shop always had a box of random vegetables that needed to be used up, so it was my job to make use of these. I had no idea about vegetarian cooking (apart from baking) and this cookery book wasn't available then. However, it was fun being creative and making up my own recipes from what was on offer.

It's handy having your own health store...

During the 1980s, interest in Dru Yoga grew quickly and so did the numbers of people visiting. I started off cooking for four or five people. This seemed to double every few months. It wasn't long before we started running yoga conferences. Starting with a hundred delegates that, too, doubled each year. Before I knew it we were providing vegetarian food for thousands of people!

For the next ten years we ran courses mostly from large houses, always amazed at how many meals we could cook from a single cooker in a domestic kitchen.

In 1997 we established our very own Dru Training Centre in North Wales, complete with commercial cookers and that blessed creation—a pass-through dishwasher.

That blessed
creation: a
pass-through
dishwasher

Anna Yoga

There's a whole branch of yoga called Anna Yoga, which literally means the 'yoga of food'. It's nothing to do with a person called Annie—'anna' is the Sanskrit word for food.

Anna Yoga, like Ayurveda, is about what and how you eat, but it places a greater emphasis on how food is first prepared and served.

Anna Yoga
isn't named
after a yoga
teacher called
Annie

PREPARING THE FOOD

Mental and emotional energy is expansive and affects not just yourself but other people as well. That's why some people have a 'wet blanket' effect when they walk into a room, while others can light up the same room with joy and enthusiasm. This same expansive energy is said to permeate the food we cook—meaning the ingredients can be tainted by misery or improved by joy and love.

Before I start cooking, I always try to create a good intention. I take a few moments to focus on my breathing and think about the people I'm cooking for. I ask myself to add love and light to the food. Then I light a candle and play some uplifting music.

When I was young and had a childhood illness, my grandmother used to give me either evaporated milk mixed with sugar and warm water, or some alcoholic 'concoction'. I now realise this may not have been the best medicine in terms of natural healing, but it was prepared with so much love and good intention that it seemed to work anyway.

SERVING THE FOOD

Another important but much underestimated Anna
Yoga principle is how the food is served. Creating a nice
environment and serving the food well goes a long way in
determining how the food tastes and how well it is digested.
A very special connection can be made between the person
giving and the person receiving the food.

JALARAM—THE FEEDING SAINT

I often travelled to India organising the food for the Dru
retreats we ran in Gujarat state. When I was in my twenties
I first heard the story of Jalaram Bapa, a 19th century saint
from a town called Virpur. He was famous for feeding the poor
and healing the sick. What I found most fascinating was that he
wasn't a phenomenon from the distant past. Jalaram passed in
1885, so at the time it was only 100 years since he'd been alive.
I even met people whose grandparents remembered him.

Jalaram's career started by his giving food away from his
father's shop free of charge. Of course this eventually got him
into trouble.

He later established his own place, giving away free meals, relying on donations of food and money. It was a struggle at first; his wife even had to sell her wedding jewellery to make ends meet, something you only ever did as a very last resort.

Jalaram's was no ordinary soup kitchen; he and his wife knew the power of love. All the meals were made with spiritual devotion. Once a man in the village had a very serious stomach complaint. He didn't know how to cure himself and had tried everything. Then he had an idea, and made a mental promise to himself that he would donate a certain amount of rice to Jalaram if he got better. He didn't mention this to Jalaram or anyone else. To his amazement he did find relief and soon returned to health. With this and similar incidents Jalaram quickly became famous. Suddenly, if anyone was sick it became a tradition to go to see him in Virpur, donate some food and ask Jalaram for help.

Jalaram was like a kindly father figure. He was called Jalaram Bapa ('bapa' means father), a bit like a Father Christmas who is generous with food rather than presents. Jalaram was a celebrity in his own lifetime but never wanted to be treated as such. When asked for advice, he always said to feed everyone with love and see God in other people. Jalaram has been my inspiration for the last 30 years, and I try to infuse love into my cooking in the same way.

Jalaram always served his favourite dish: curried potato with kitcheri and kadhi (a special sauce made from yoghurt). Eat it with love and think of the miracles that happen every day.

JALARAM
TEMPLE
જલારામ
મંદિર
1
૧
જ્ય જલારામ
ગેસ્ટ હાઉસ
C, NON, A/C. DELUX ROOM'S.
ચોક, વિરપુર [જલારામ] મો:૦૨૮૨૫૯૧૧૮૮૩

Jalaram's Kitcheri

This is like the kitcheri that Jalaram made. It's a very simple, economical
but nutritious dish. Every day this dish is served to hundreds of people
who visit Jalaram's temple in his home town of Virpur in Gujarat.

Serves 2

75 g basmati rice

50 g split mung beans

400 ml water

¼ tsp salt

pinch of black pepper

¼ tsp ground turmeric

½ tsp cumin seeds

1 tbsp chopped fresh coriander

2 tsp ghee

½ tsp grated fresh ginger

½ lemon *juiced*

Wash the rice and mung beans thoroughly several times.

In a medium pan, mix the rice, mung beans, black pepper,
turmeric, ginger and water. Bring to the boil then turn the
heat down to low, cover the pot and let the kitcheri cook for
30 minutes.

Stir occasionally to make sure the mixture is not sticking at
the bottom. Add a little more water if it dries out. It should
have a porridge-like consistency when cooked.

Melt the ghee in a pan until it becomes clear. Add the cumin
seeds and stir until the aroma is released (about 1 minute)
then mix into the kitcheri.

Add the salt, lemon juice and coriander. Stir gently until
well-mixed.

Serve with Kadhi Sauce.

Kadhi Sauce

This yoghurt sauce, popular in Gujarat, is traditionally served with Jalaram's kitcheri. Yoghurt is fermented, which makes it sour but also easier to digest than normal milk—hence its popularity in Ayurvedic cooking.

Serves 2

250 ml water

1 tbsp gram flour

75 ml live yoghurt

1 tsp ghee

¼ tsp black mustard seeds

¼ tsp grated fresh ginger

pinch of chilli powder

pinch of asafoetida

¼ tsp ground turmeric

½ tsp jaggery

½ lemon *juiced*

½ tsp salt

Whisk the gram flour, yoghurt and 50 ml of the water till smooth. Boil the remaining water, and slowly whisk into the yoghurt mix. Heat the ghee in a pan, add the mustard seeds and cover. Cook until they splutter.

When most have crackled, remove from the heat.

Add the fresh ginger and powdered spices. Mix well.

Allow to cool a little then stir in the yoghurt mix.

Gently reheat and stir as you bring the mixture to the boil.

Reduce the heat, and then stir in the lemon, salt and jaggery. Simmer for a few minutes and keep stirring.

Serve warm with Kitcheri.

Gujarati Alu Sak

This recipe is thickened with gram (chick pea) flour which is
gluten-free and high in protein.

Serves 2-4

500 g potatoes *peeled, cubed & steamed*	Combine the yoghurt, water and gram flour in a bowl and beat well to remove any lumps.
100 ml live yoghurt	Heat the ghee in a pan and add the mustard seeds and cover. When they crackle and pop, remove from the heat and let the pan cool slightly.
100 ml water	
2 tsp gram flour	
1 tbsp butter ghee	Add the rest of the seeds, bay leaf, cloves and cinnamon stick.
¼ tsp black mustard seeds	
½ tsp cumin seeds	Replace on the heat and stir gently for a few seconds.
½ tsp fennel seeds	Remove from the heat again and mix in the powdered spices. Replace on the heat, stir for a few seconds.
¼ tsp black onion seeds	
1 bay leaf	Add the yoghurt mix while stirring continuously.
2 cloves	Bring to the boil.
1 cm stick cinnamon	Stir in the steamed potatoes and salt.
pinch of asafoetida	Garnish with fresh coriander.
¼ tsp chilli powder	
¼ tsp ground turmeric	
½ tsp ground coriander	
1 tbsp chopped fresh coriander	
salt *to taste*	

Prana

Prana is the Sanskrit word for the vital energy that is present in all living things, including food. Not normally considered when discussing nutrition, it is in fact an essential component of what we eat—the food's own living energy. The most prana can be found in fresh, living food. It is said to be related closely to the sun's energy from which it came, through the process of photosynthesis.

Anna Yoga describes three types of food. *Sattvic* food is pure, healthy and full of nutrients and vitality. *Rajasic* food is overly spiced, salted or too oily. It stimulates the senses, but ultimately causes ill health. And finally there is *tamasic* food which is dead, low in nutrients and devoid of prana.

The prana levels in food are also influenced by the cook. In Ayurveda they even recommend having a healthy person prepare your food.

An excellent way to increase the prana in your body is through the practice of pranayama, which is a series of yogic breathing techniques. My favourite is nadi shodhana or 'alternate nostril breath'. It balances the left and right sides of the brain and is really calming and relaxing. (If you have high blood pressure, check with a yoga teacher before performing any pranayama.)

Nadi Shodhana

ALTERNATE NOSTRIL BREATH

> Close your left nostril by pressing with your little finger just below the bony ridge of your nose. Breathe in through your right nostril.

> Place your thumb against the right nostril to close it as you release the pressure of your little finger against your left nostril. Breathe out through your left nostril.

> Keeping your thumb and little finger where they are, breathe in through the left nostril.

> Release the pressure of your thumb against your right nostril while at the same time pressing your little finger against your left nostril to close it. Breathe out through the right nostril.

Continue to follow the four stages in the cycle, opening and closing your nostrils as described. Breathe gently and naturally without strain. You may find that you can only perform a few consecutive rounds to begin with. Practise the technique regularly until you can maintain an even, steady alternate nostril breath for up to five minutes.

Fresh foods have the most prana, particularly if they are raw. Ideally every main meal should have a raw or lightly cooked component. Bean sprouts as a food are particularly high in prana as they are still growing. They are easy to grow at home and make a great snack or sprinkle. They are also easily digested and high in protein.

However, the best way to get a good hit of prana through your diet is to juice vegetables. Drinking vegetable juice can give you the energy and vitality from an entire bunch of carrots, a whole beetroot and half a head of celery in a single, easy to drink glassful. Try a fresh vegetable juice for yourself and you can really feel its power being absorbed.

A quick word about microwaves. A microwave can be convenient to reheat or defrost something quickly. But be aware that the rays disrupt the prana in the food and destroy its vitality. So use it sparingly, if at all.

My advice is to get a vegetable juicer and use it as often as you can

Vegetarian Food

At the Dru centres, all the food is vegetarian to help complement a healthy lifestyle. You don't necessarily need to be a strict vegetarian to be healthy though. Even a predominantly plant-based diet is a much healthier lifestyle choice than eating largely animal products every day.

In the USA, a congregation called 'Seventh Day Adventists' has many people who choose to be vegetarian. Other than their diet, their environment and lifestyle are similar to those of the non-vegetarians in the same congregation. Both groups were the basis of a scientific study. (Orlich, Fraser & Gray, 2014)

Overall, the study concluded that:

> the vegetarians and vegans
> were found to be less likely to
> suffer from heart disease
> and cancer

> vegetarians had less
> gastro-intestinal cancer
> (i.e. colon cancer, pancreatic cancer,
> liver cancer, stomach cancer), especially
> among lacto-ovo-vegetarians

> vegan women experienced fewer
> female-specific cancers.

VEGETARIAN PROTEIN SOURCES

PULSES

A meat-free meal basically requires replacing meat with vegetable protein. The best plant-based protein sources are pulses (beans and lentils), although many people tend to be a bit wary of them, thinking you have to be up all night soaking them. Yes, some beans do need soaking but you don't have to stand there watching them! In the Dru kitchen, we use mainly split pulses such as split lentils and split peas because they cook more quickly, or small pulses such as mung or adzuki beans.

Some people also worry that pulses are indigestible and cause bloating. This can be a problem, but the secret is to really cook them well so that the indigestible elements break down properly. These are mainly carbohydrates or starch, which are chains of sugar molecules. Cooking breaks them into shorter chains, making them more digestible and slightly sweeter to the taste. They are broken down further in your mouth where the digestive enzyme amylase continues the process. Another good reason not to eat too fast!

I have included some Ayurvedic recipes which use herbs and spices to help make pulses more digestible.

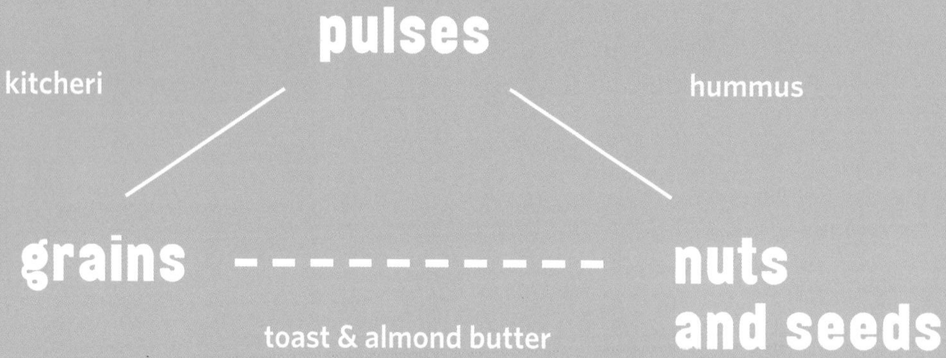

———————   **well-matched proteins**

– – – – – –   **less well-matched proteins**

CREATING COMPLETE PROTEINS

The next thing to remember, when eating more vegetarian food, is that pulses in themselves are not a complete protein. In fact, some of the amino acids (the component parts of protein) can be in short supply. This is also the case for most proteins found in grains, nuts and seeds. Mother Nature has made it easy though; you can simply combine them. When combined, grains, seeds, nuts and pulses form complete proteins, and provide the right balance of amino acids for our needs.

The best combination of grains and pulses is normally in a 2:1 ratio, which is in fact the basic diet of a lot of cultures: for example 'rice and lentils' in India, 'corn and beans' in the Americas, 'pitta bread and hummus' in the Middle East and our very own British 'baked beans on toast'.

The good news is you don't need a degree in nutrition to eat a healthy vegetarian diet. This combination of grains and pulses provides a really good balance of protein and carbohydrate.

Using nuts and seeds as a vegetable protein source has the added benefit of providing omega-3 essential fatty acids, which can be deficient in a lot of Western diets. Again, nuts and seeds make a complete protein when mixed with pulses and/or grains. Using all three together is a sort of 'belt and braces' approach.

Keith's protein mantra: eat whole grains with half the amount of pulses and a sprinkling of nuts and seeds

Dairy products in moderation are a good source of protein. Ayurvedic recipes often include yoghurt, ghee, and one of our favourite ingredients, paneer.

A cow's diet greatly affects the nutrient content of her milk so whenever possible get your milk, cream, butter and cheeses from free-range, grass-fed cows.

The oil in green grass contains 50% omega-3 essential fatty acids and cows normally eat a lot of grass. They filter out the omega-3 and transfer it to their milk. Nowadays, to increase production, cattle are often kept indoors and fed corn and soya, both lacking in omega-3.

Another great source of protein is eggs, best when they are organic and from free-range, grass-fed chickens

KEFIR

Kefir made from milk is another excellent source of protein. It is made like yoghurt, by fermenting milk with probiotic bacteria. But unlike yoghurt the beneficial bacteria in kefir will actually colonise your gut with healthy gut flora (microbes living in your intestine), whereas yoghurt will only help sustain what is already there.

Gut flora are very important. The right ones help create a healthy environment in your digestive tract. But the wrong gut flora hinder digestion. Undigested food creates toxins, no matter how healthily you eat.

Good gut flora are a bit like Boy Scouts or Girl Guides on 'Bob-a-Job Week'. Keen and helpful, they will tidy up your digestive tract and help repair it, always putting your needs before theirs. The bad bugs are more like unwelcome house guests who eat up all your nice food, create a mess and never clear up. Worst of all, they're hard to get rid of!

Eating kefir is like sending bus-loads of eager Scouts and Guides into your digestive system. Their energetic cleaning, with mops and brooms, will disturb the lethargy of the unwelcome bacteria, who will soon decide to leave.

Eating kefir is like sending bus-loads of eager Boy Scouts and Girl Guides into your digestive system to clean it up.

You can make your own kefir from a starter which is normally a walnut-sized lump of white grains. These are not grains in the conventional sense, but small cultures of yeasts and lactic acid bacteria. It's possible to make subsequent batches of kefir from the first one, but in practice you may need a new starter culture each time. Luckily, you can now buy great ready-made kefir from many health shops.

People who can't digest milk or are lactose intolerant can sometimes eat kefir, as the lactose is converted to lactic acid by the cultures. Kefir can also be made from goats' milk or non-dairy milks such as soya, hemp, almond or coconut. In fact, kefir is so versatile it can even be made from sweetened water.

Kefir is derived from the Turkish word 'keyif' meaning 'feeling good', and is thought to have originated in present-day Georgia. This is an area linking Russia, Turkey and Iran. It has been used in these countries for hundreds of years as a popular health drink, and all kinds of health benefits are attributed to kefir.

CARBOHYDRATES

In the Ayurvedic traditions there are said to be six different tastes: sweet, salty, sour, astringent, bitter and pungent. Carbohydrates form the basis of the sweet taste, which is considered to be the most important. Sweet is present in most of our food and is the first taste we experience in our mother's milk. Sweet is also the first taste that nature produces in photosynthesis in the form of glucose.

There are three main types of carbohydrates in our food: **sugars**, **oligosaccharides** and **polysaccharides**.

The sugars come in either single molecules (monosaccharide) or in pairs (disaccharide). Both types are soluble in water, form crystals when dehydrated and taste sweet.

Monosaccharides are the basic building blocks of all other carbohydrates. The most common are glucose (produced by all plants), fructose (found in fruit and honey) and galactose (found in milk). The main disaccharide pairs are sucrose (glucose + fructose), lactose found in milk (glucose + galactose) and maltose (two glucose sugars joined together).

Longer chains of three to nine sugars are called oligosaccharides from the Greek 'oligos', meaning a few. Oligosaccharides are found naturally in some vegetables and are used as a food sweetener. One example is maltodextrin which is used to make beer, and is a high-energy food for athletes. It can have up to 20 glucose molecules in a chain. In general, the shorter the chain the sweeter the taste.

If a carbohydrate has more than nine sugars it is called a polysaccharide. The most important of these is starch which is common in many foods. Plants store glucose in this way by creating these long chains. They can be made up of hundreds or even thousands of sugars.

Starchy foods like grains, pulses and some vegetables get sweeter as we chew or cook them. The amylase in our saliva starts breaking the starch into shorter chains, releasing sugars as we chew. That's why it's so important to chew food well—digestion starts in the mouth. Brown rice is said to change flavour ten times as it gets progressively sweeter if you chew it for long enough.

The longer starch chains are digested more slowly; it's a bit like unravelling a piece of string. It also depends on how much the starch is encased in the structure of food. Wholegrains digest slowly as they are coated with a husk and are very fibrous. Grinding and refining grains into flour breaks down their structure and means sugar is released more quickly. This is quantified as the food's 'GI index' which indicates how quickly different foods release sugar into our bloodstream. This index is calculated as a percentage; the higher the GI, the more quickly the sugar is released from the food.

The other consideration in sugar metabolism is related to the nutrient content of the food. With refined products like sugar or white flour, our body does not have all the cofactors it needs to use the sugar properly (such as minerals and vitamins). The only option is to turn the sugar into fat, not because we have eaten too much food, but because this is the only way our body can process it. That's why 'junk foods' are so fattening, and can make you overweight but still malnourished.

Nature hasn't made any mistakes—natural grains come packaged with all the nutrients and enzymes you need so you can digest them. It's like a toolkit that helps you to dismantle each grain properly.

Digesting carbohydrates is a bit like going through immigration control at an airport. If there's a plane full of unrefined complex carbohydrates they arrive at passport control in an orderly manner and with all the right documents. That means the officials can deal with them easily and accurately, and they flow efficiently through the system.

In contrast, when a plane full of sugar or refined carbohydrates arrives there is no control. These foods don't have the right documents (or nutrients) to be processed properly. Everyone is trying to rush through at the same time, and the system is overloaded. Many of them can't be dealt with straight away so they are sent to a holding area—which in the body means they are converted into fat. It's total chaos, and the whole system is stressed.

The carbohydrates which are found in whole grains, fruit and vegetables are locked into the structure of the food. It takes time for them to be digested. And just like well-organised immigration, they release sugar into your system slowly and safely.

ANTIOXIDANTS

A popular debate these days is to compare the energy efficiency of photosynthesis in plants with that of solar panels. Some claim that solar panels are now more efficient than nature at turning sunlight into energy. But I think plants win hands down. First of all there's the beauty of their design; compare an exquisite sun-dappled forest with a solar panel. Next, plants are self-repairing and self-replicating. And thirdly, plants store energy in complex ways: as sugars, starches and cellulose, as well as in structured fibres like wood.

Photosynthesis is an extremely complex and powerful chemical reaction. In fact, it's so powerful that plants need to create a safety net in the form of antioxidants to mop up excess energy which could otherwise damage the plant cells. Antioxidants act a bit like the cooling rods in a nuclear reactor.

In our metabolism the digestion of food is as energetic as photosynthesis in plants. Oxygen is used to turn sugars back into energy and carbon dioxide. So we need our own army of antioxidants to control this process. Unfortunately, and unlike most other animals, we humans can't produce vitamin C which is an important antioxidant. So we have colour vision instead. The bright colours in fruits and vegetables indicate the presence of antioxidants, so it's no coincidence that we are one of the few mammals that can see colour—which enables us to find colourful, antioxidant-rich foods.

Our modern lifestyle with its stress and exposure to chemical pollutants produces a lot of toxic particles (free radicals) in our bodies and they can only be eliminated by antioxidants. So it's more important than ever to eat fresh fruit and vegetables every day.

There is a beautiful symbiosis between plants and humans. Plants exhale oxygen, which we inhale. We exhale carbon dioxide, which the plants breathe back in again. To fully experience this wonder of nature, try my short meditation.

BREATH OF LIFE MEDITATION

PART 1 **EASY**

Stand in a leafy forest or near some trees. As you breathe in, smell the cool sweetness of the air and feel your feet on the earth. Sense a connection with the trees and inhale the energy-enriched air from their leaves. Allow that to fill your lungs and feel gratitude towards the plants around you.

Exhale the carbon-rich air from your lungs while at the same time adding your love and energy to it. Imagine the trees around you breathing it in and then exhaling their oxygen-rich air back to you.

PART 2 **ADVANCED**

Imagine the space in your lungs as an upside-down tree: the trachea as the trunk, the bronchi as the branches, and alveoli as the leaves and buds. Trees are living matter surrounded by space, while your lungs are space surrounded by living matter. Just like male and female, they are beautifully opposite and wholly compatible.

The in-breath is like a breeze flowing through you, gently filling the alveoli with fresh, cool air. On the out-breath be aware of the warm carbon-rich air leaving you, and imagine it moving up through a tall tree towering above you. It wafts through the leaves and now the tree breathes. Then visualise the cool, moist, oxygen-rich air circulating back towards you. Inhaling, feel the fresh air flowing through you again. Repeat the cycle two or three times.

FATS & OILS

THE GOOD, THE BAD AND THE UGLY

Knowing which fats and oils to eat (and which to avoid) has become ever more confusing with so many different opinions having been expressed over the last few decades.

I remember being told to eat margarine instead of butter. Then to avoid all saturated fats and to use refined, polyunsaturated fats instead. But now we're told that butter is better than margarine after all!

It might help to think of fats as The Good, the Bad and the Ugly. Like the film of the same name, the Good are not always well-behaved. The Bad can sometimes be good, but the Ugly can be relied on to be truly wicked!

IN A NUTSHELL

In a nutshell means literally that. Natural fats and oils should be stored away from heat, light and air to prevent them from deteriorating. Nature inherently provides a perfect storage system for these fats and oils: within the nuts and seeds themselves. When undisturbed, they will stay fresh for a long time.

Oxidation changes Good oils to Bad

Although it's healthy to eat plenty of nuts and seeds, they can be tough and need a lot of chewing. Soaking overnight helps to soften them, and it also activates their enzymes and makes them more alive and digestible. Every evening I soak some whole almonds so that by the morning they are plump, juicy and easy to peel. It's a good idea to remove almond skins as they contain indigestible tannins that protect the nut (part of the storage system). My soaked almonds are then easy to chop and are delicious in my breakfast.

Another way to make fresh nuts and seeds easier to eat is to grind them in a food processor, or crush them in a pestle and mortar. Once ground, you should eat the nuts/seeds straight away because the oils oxidise fairly quickly once they become exposed to light and air. Oxidation changes Good oils to Bad.

Eating fresh nuts and seeds is an excellent way to get our essential fatty acids, but we still need other types of fats and oils for cooking, salad dressings and for topical applications.

THE GOOD OILS

The only Good oils are those that are termed 'virgin' or 'extra virgin' or 'unrefined cold pressed'. When fresh, these contain essential fatty acids, nutrients and antioxidants.

Unsaturated oils, however, are still unstable and will oxidise quickly when exposed to the atmosphere—even if they are cold-pressed and virgin. To stay fresh, they need to be stored in a cool, dark place such as the fridge. Don't cook with unsaturated oils because heat damages them and creates free radicals. These are very bad news—they cause massive damage to our cells and tissues. Use unsaturated oils raw instead, as dressings on salads, or poured as a sauce on hot food. When served on a plate, the food will not be hot enough to damage the oil—which will instead help to moisten the food and lubricate the meal.

Extra virgin olive oil is monounsaturated. It's a bit more heat stable than polyunsaturated oils, which means it's good for light cooking. Try to avoid letting olive oil get too hot in the pan as this damages the fatty acids. It's best to put any vegetables in first, then add the oil. The moisture in the vegetables helps control the temperature in the pan.

Saturated fats are better for serious cooking where you need more heat—for example cooking whole spices. The best cooking oil is coconut oil: virgin, cold-pressed and stored in a glass container. Coconut oil has shorter fatty acid chains, making it easier to digest. Butter ghee is the other fat you can use for cooking. Ghee is highly prized in Ayurveda, not just for cooking, but also as a solvent for medicinal preparations.

ESSENTIAL FATTY ACIDS

We humans can create fatty acids out of the sugars and oils that we eat. But there are two fatty acids that we can't make ourselves. These are the omega-6 and omega-3 essential fatty acids. They are called 'essential' because it's essential that we include them in our diet. It's not just about getting enough of each though—they need to be eaten in the correct ratio, which is approximately 5:1 (so for every 5 grams of pure omega-6 you need to consume 1 gram of pure omega-3).

Omega-6 and omega-3 are very similar, so they compete for the same enzymes and metabolic pathways. When it comes to metabolising fats, the body works on a 'first come, first served' basis. So if you eat too much omega-6, it will prevent you from absorbing enough omega-3, and vice versa.

Unfortunately, Western diets often have over 15 times more omega-6 fatty acids than omega-3. This excess of omega-6 creates a deficit in the amount of omega-3 that we can absorb, and exacerbates the problem. So although omega-6 is a good fat, having too much changes it from good to bad.

WHEN GOOD OILS BECOME BAD

Imagine people queuing up to enter a popular nightclub.

As we need a 5:1 omega balance ratio, let's say that five omega-6s represent one boy, and one omega-3 represents one girl.

Of course it's best when there are equal numbers of boys and girls. Then they can be let in as they arrive. But if there are more boys in the queue than girls, there's a gender imbalance that could lead to trouble later on. And the security guards would need to allow more girls in to restore the balance.

For us, too much omega-6 is linked to chronic conditions like arthritis and other forms of inflammation. The only way we can restore the balance is by letting more omega-3 girls into our nightclub.

THE UGLY

In our metabolic nightclub, we can see the problem that arises if we have too many good guys (omega-6 fats). They're sure to misbehave if there aren't enough omega-3 fats around to keep them happy.

But there are other fats that are much, much worse.

Fats that go looking for trouble!

These are the 'gangland' type of fatty acids that roar up on their motorcycles, gate-crashing our nightclub and starting to pick fights with the other visitors. They're the troublesome refined, polyunsaturated fats that have had all their natural goodness taken away.

If we use these polyunsaturated fats for cooking, they become unstable and oxidise into highly energetic free radicals. In the nightclub, the free radicals are so agitated that they start breaking chairs and smashing glasses just for fun!

THE TRULY UGLY...

Worse still are the refined oils that have been hydrogenated. These are the sneakiest by far, because they enter by stealth. They hide in delicious-looking pastries, cakes, cookies and chocolate. These hydrogenated fats are so clever that the foods baked using them turn out even better than when their healthy, natural saturated fatty brethren are used. In fact, they are so tempting that we welcome them in huge crowds. They come in many of the convenience foods we love to eat: cereals at breakfast, snack bars during a break, bread at lunchtime and pies in the evening.

Even our bodies are tricked—they simply don't recognise these unnatural, synthetic fats. These hydrogenated fats have different molecular structures from those of natural fats, but our bodies have not adapted to spotting the difference.

Imagine both hydrogenated and natural fats wearing trenchcoats in differing shades of beige: light beige and dark beige. The security guards in our metabolic nightclub wear sunglasses, even though it's night-time, so they have trouble telling the different fats apart.

Hydrogenated fats are like sleeper agents. They seem harmless, melding themselves into the very fabric of our being, just waiting to carry out an atrocious act. Somehow our bodies have been totally fooled by these smooth and charming ingredients, unaware of the hidden dangers. Once admitted, these synthetic fats create havoc in our cells.

Fats are used to build important cell structures like cell walls and membranes. In a way it is similar to the dry stone walls we have here in Wales. A good builder, with the right type of stones, can create a strong wall without needing cement—a wall that can withstand the gales and storms we get here. He will cast aside any ill-fitting or bad stones.

If you only ever provide the builder with rough misshapen rocks, the quality and strength of the wall will be poor. In the same way, our bodies need good fats as building blocks. Poor building materials lead to weaker tissues and faulty metabolism.

AVOID THE UGLY FATS

Sensible adults tend to stay away from the rough part of town on a Saturday night (especially if the local football team has just lost). In the same way, it's best to avoid refined oils and hydrogenated fats if you can. Use virgin, cold-pressed oils for dressings and saturated oils like butter, ghee or virgin coconut oil for cooking.

GETTING ENOUGH OF THE GOOD

The omega-6 essential fatty acids are quite common in the foods we normally eat, so getting enough of them is not normally an issue. The problem is that modern diets are lacking in essential omega-3 oils.

A great solution is to use linseed oil. This is particularly high in omega-3, and helps restore the healthy balance between omega-6 and omega-3. Other good sources are hemp, chia and pumpkin oils. They do get damaged by heat, light and air though, so don't use them for cooking. Make sure they are totally fresh, unrefined and supplied in a dark bottle. Store them in the fridge or in a cool place away from light. Consume them daily so that you don't keep them for too long, and try to use them up within a few weeks. At home I use Udo's Oil, which is produced in an air-free environment, packaged in a dark bottle and kept refrigerated until it is sold.

The freshest source of oil though, and also the cheapest by far, is straight from the seed. Linseeds are 50% oil, but they have a tough shell and are totally indigestible when eaten whole. The best thing to do is grind them and then eat them straight away. Make sure you are getting plenty of fluids as linseeds absorb a lot of water.

MAKING THE GOOD EVEN BETTER

Once we've sorted out our metabolic nightclub by keeping out the ugly fats, and we have the right balance of omega-3 and omega-6, the romance and magic can really start. With the right numbers of boys and girls and no troublemakers, we can create the conditions we need for a wonderful transformation.

Given the right conditions, a healthy person converts about 20% of the omega-3 oils they consume into another fatty acid called eicosapentaenoic acid (EPA). This is a very useful fat in the body, and produces a prostaglandin (PGE3) that reduces inflammation and blood clotting.

But it doesn't stop there. The love continues in a wonderful alchemy to produce docosahexaenoic acid (DHA). Our brain and eyes need DHA like good muscles need protein.

It's always best to fall in love naturally—but there's no harm in helping things along. Getting enough omega-3 fats in your food starts the process, but it's a good idea to supplement your diet with EPA and DHA. They are found in marine algae or fish that eat them. Or, of course, in fish that eat the fish that eat the algae. Famously, fish oil has been the main supplement for EPA and DHA, but now you can cut out the middle man (or middle fish)! Vegan supplements which contain the oils extracted directly from the algae are now available. If you want to know more, Udo Erasmus has written a fantastic book called *Fats that Heal and Fats that Kill.*

**It's always best to fall in love naturally,
but there's no harm in helping things along.**

Fellow Ayurveda
course tutors
Mansukh and
Shona

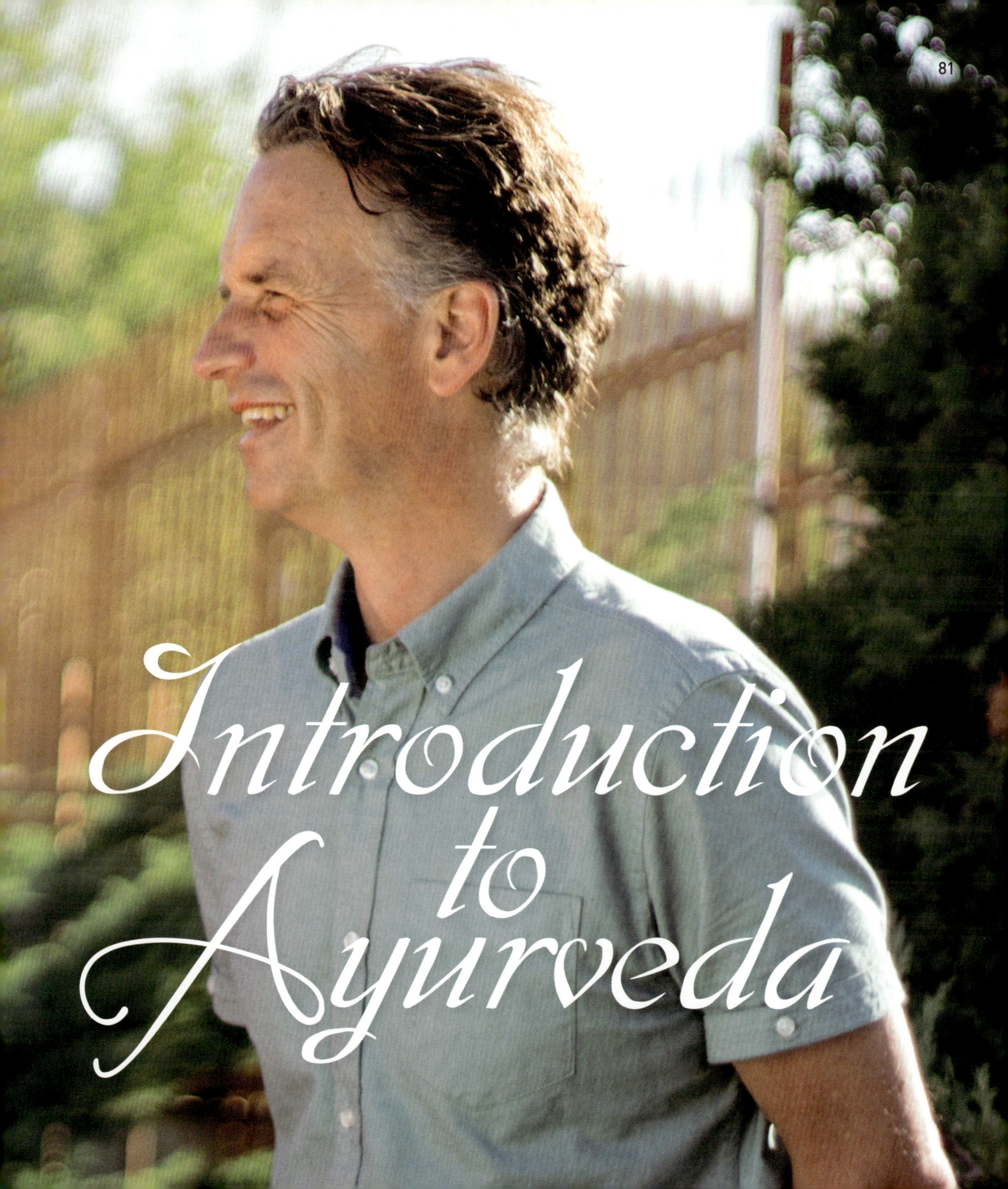

Introduction to Ayurveda

Ayurveda is an ancient medical system used alongside yoga to create health and wellbeing, so naturally I use a lot of Ayurvedic principles in my cooking. Some of these principles are quite simple, and just plain old common sense.

For years, whenever I visited India I would see an Ayurvedic doctor called Dr Gupta. He told me most of the western people who come to him want complicated herbal remedies, diet lists or in-depth therapies—when most of the health problems he encounters are caused by people simply staying up too late, eating at the wrong time or eating in a hurry. 'I make my living from Westerners who skip lunch!' he joked. With Ayurveda, you can benefit a lot by just getting the basics right first.

1 COOK WITH LOVE

It's important how the food is cooked and served.

When I first started cooking, I quickly realised that my emotional state determined how the food turned out. If I was agitated no-one liked my cooking—but when I was happy everybody loved it! Having the right intention really makes a big difference. Spending a few minutes relaxing, or focusing on your breathing, really helps to put you in the right mood to create a wonderful meal.

2 EAT AT A REGULAR TIME

Have three main meals a day—breakfast, lunch and supper.

Eat at regular times and without snacking (too much). It is better if the evening meal is the lightest meal and eaten before 7.30pm. Traditionally in Ayurveda it's important to eat lunch around midday, when the sun's fire energy, and therefore our digestive fire, is strongest. However, if you don't have time for a large lunch, try eating a bigger breakfast. The rule of thumb is to eat breakfast like a king, lunch like a prince (or the other way round) and supper like a pauper.

I meet a lot of people who skip breakfast, but fuel up on coffee and eat a rushed lunch. They then fill up with unhealthy snacks and have a large meal quite late in the evening. Even if the food is of good quality, this lifestyle sows the seeds of ill health. The great thing about Ayurveda is that it is as much about prevention as cure. For your long-term health, *when* you eat is just as important as *what* you eat.

3 EAT SLOWLY

Savour your food—eat slowly and with awareness. It can be a real meditation to enjoy all the flavours. By eating more slowly and with awareness, I find I eat less. Somehow a lot of us have a habit of eating too fast and then end up eating too much. This is because the 'full' reflex seems to take a while to kick in. It's easy to eat too much before your body is ready to tell you to stop. I savour every mouthful and deliberately eat a bit less than I think I want to.

4 BE RELAXED AS YOU EAT

You should try to relax as you eat. If you are stressed, you just can't digest or absorb the food properly. Stress means adrenaline, which keeps your body at a sustained level of 'fight or flight'. This is bad news as it pulls the blood supply away from your digestive system. In the short term it can lead to poor absorption and indigestion, and in the long term to more serious digestive problems. Eat quietly, or enjoy a pleasant conversation. The worst thing you can do is to have a big argument as you eat—this just seems to turn the food into poison. No matter if the food is the healthiest possible, it'll still give you indigestion. Best to reschedule an argument to an hour or so after the meal, to give your food time to be digested properly. Better still, find a way to resolve your conflict without resorting to an argument!

5 EAT ADEQUATELY

Just as important is how much you eat. In traditional Ayurveda, they say you should fill your stomach with one third food, one third liquid and leave one third empty for air. In practice, try not to overeat and stop just before you feel full. Your stomach is a bit like your washing machine; if you cram it too full it can't work properly.

6 EAT ACCORDING TO YOUR CONSTITUTION

In Ayurveda there are three doshas: vata, pitta and kapha. Each person's constitution is said to be made up of a specific combination of these three doshas—making us all unique.

In brief, a creative person is said to have a lot of vata in their constitution and needs to eat nourishing and warm food regularly. A dynamic person is said to have a lot of pitta and needs a lot of fresh and healthy food. And a sturdy person is said to have a lot of kapha in their constitution and should avoid eating too much heavy food.

Funnily enough, we all seem to be drawn to do the exact opposite of what is good for us. Luckily a little knowledge of Ayurveda will develop a self-awareness that can help you choose the food that is right for you.

THE THREE DOSHAS

The idea of constitution types is not necessarily exclusive to Ayurveda. Indeed, traditional Chinese medicine has a similar system based on five elements: wood, fire, earth, metal and water. Until the 1800s, Western medicine was founded on the four humours, which originated in Greek and Roman philosophy.

All of these systems recognise that people are unique and have individual needs based on the balance of elements within them.

VATA DOSHA

The vata dosha is composed of air and space. We already recognise
this and may think of a person as being 'airy', 'full of air' or things
may be 'up in the air'.

People who have an air constitution are actually very creative, with a
lot of space in their minds. They might be artistic or good musicians.
They are intelligent and love learning new things. When balanced,
vata types are enthusiastic, good talkers and happy.

Physically, they tend to be slim, whether tall or short. Often vata types
have dark hair which tends to be curly. Air is a dry constitution, so
their skin and hair may be drier than usual.

Of all the constitutions, vata types have the most variable digestion
and really need to eat regularly with easy-to-digest food. The paradox
is that they are the most likely to be distracted, skip a meal, or even
forget to eat!

This is where an awareness of the doshas becomes useful. In
Ayurveda they say 'like attracts like'. So a person whose system is
unbalanced will tend to do more of the things that make it worse,
and less of what would be of benefit. For example, an overly stressed
person sometimes doesn't feel like resting or eating.

The main indication of vata imbalance is worry or fear. Abdominal bloating is another sign that their digestion is stressed and not working properly. Unbalanced vata types will also start talking very fast and jump from one subject to another.

Modern TV programmes tend to be very vata, with presenters moving quickly and enthusiastically from one topic to the next. Journalism or the performing arts suit people with a vata constitution.

Vata types have high energy, but this tends to be in short bursts. They can burn out quickly, particularly if their food intake is irregular, or if they don't get enough sleep. They are the most prone to insomnia, waking in the early hours, still tired but unable to get back to sleep.

Vata types have high energy, but this tends to be in short bursts and they can burn out quickly.

Vata

How to **unbalance** vata

- Worry, be anxious about the future, think about what could go wrong.

- Regularly skip meals, go on a fast or eat lots of raw foods in winter.

- Avoid routine, change your work and eating patterns every day.

- Eat in a hurry or on the move, snack on cold dry foods.

- Rush around, running from place to place.

- Take long-distance journeys, especially by airplane.

- Work late on computers and other electronic devices; stay up past midnight.

- Over-indulge in alcohol and refined or sugary foods.

- Take on a very stressful job, or night-shift work.

How to **balance** vata

- Be positive and enthusiastic, but get enough rest.

- Eat regular, nourishing meals.

- Follow a daily Ayurvedic routine; practise dinacharya.

- Have a regular body massage with oil.

- Be in the moment; focus on the task at hand.

- Wind down in the evening with yoga and relaxation; try to get 8 hours sleep.

- Eat warm, moist foods; emphasise sweet, sour and salty tastes in your food.

- Practise yoga and meditation to recharge your creativity.

- Wrap up warm and walk in nature.

- Look after yourself; express your feelings and needs.

PITTA DOSHA

The pitta dosha is composed of 90% fire and 10% water, so it's easier to think of it as a fire constitution. If you think of someone or something as 'fiery', or you say 'there was a lot of fire in that meeting', you could be talking about the pitta dosha at work.

Physically, pitta types can look the part with fair, red or ginger hair and a ruddy complexion. They have a medium, strong, athletic build and tend to be fit and active. They are often good at sport and enjoy competition.

People with a lot of fire are intelligent, with a sharp and discriminating mind. They are often good managers and organisers. They are perceptive, can judge people's strengths, give them appropriate tasks and motivate others. They are also very determined, and they will make sure things happen and are done properly.

They tend to be good at communicating and they make excellent public speakers. In contrast to vata types, who communicate fast, pitta types will tend to be clearer and more precise in their communication.

When pitta types get stressed they tend to overheat, feeling physically hot and bothered. Whereas the negative side of vata is worry, that of pitta is impatience and anger. They are often successful and can be very generous. Pitta types are naturally witty, thanks to their powers of good observation; however, unbalanced wit can sometimes turn to sarcasm.

In contrast to vata types—who like starting things but can get distracted and leave projects unfinished—pitta types can be very focused and driven and like to see things through to the end. Whereas the strength of vata is creativity and innovation, that of pitta is getting things done.

Pitta types have a strong digestion and good appetite. They are the one dosha type that naturally feels hungry near mealtimes. It is important that they eat regular, good quality meals so that the digestive energy is utilised. Unfortunately though, they can be so focused on tasks that they ignore the urge to eat—at which point they can become very irritable, even bad-tempered. If you are a pitta type it is important to recognise this and maintain a healthy eating pattern.

Like attracts like, so pitta types may be drawn to eat very rich or spicy food and too much meat. They may also drink too much coffee and/or alcohol. Their strong digestion can deal with it, but long term it will have a negative effect on their health, which may then fail in middle age.

The pitta dosha is the only one that is hot. Vata and kapha types both feel the cold. When indoors, vatas and kaphas will be turning the heating thermostat up, whereas the pittas will be opening all the windows!

Generally, pitta types are good organisers. They are perceptive, good at judging people's strengths, motivating them and giving them appropriate tasks.

How to **unbalance** pitta

- Fuel your activity with plenty of alcohol and coffee.

- Eat lots of rich and spicy food.

- Engage with frustrating and inefficient activities or people.

- Wear tight, warm clothing even on a hot day.

- Drive around fast in a powerful sports car.

- Exercise when you are too hot or hungry.

- Get angry with people; tell them what you really think.

- Be tough on yourself; compete with everyone.

- Work late at night; sleep less than six hours a night.

- Wear bright red or yellow clothing.

How to **balance** pitta

- Enjoy the natural tastes of fresh fruits and vegetables.

- Eat naturally sweet and bitter foods.

- Show gratitude and support other people; be a good leader.

- Wear loose clothing made from natural fibres like cotton, linen and silk.

- Get plenty of fresh air; enjoy walks in nature.

- Practise yoga; do a relaxation every day.

- Listen to others; be a good friend.

- Keep hydrated with adequate water; drink linseed tea (page 159).

- Take a relaxing massage with coconut oil.

- Drink aloe vera juice or coconut water as a cooling tonic.

KAPHA DOSHA

Kapha is an equal mix of earth and water elements, but we think of it as earth. We already recognise this type of person in phrases such as 'salt of the earth', 'down to earth' and 'grounded'.

Kapha constitution types are different from vata and pitta in that they don't get stressed easily and are generally content and easy-going. Like pitta types, they are strong but generally with a heavier build and more stamina and endurance. As in the tortoise (kapha) and hare (vata) story, slow and steady wins the race.

Kapha types are naturally hydrated and do not need to drink as much as the fire and air types. Their skin is cool, soft and moist and they are generally the most attractive of all the dosha types. Kaphas like peace and quiet, so they are the least talkative of the three, tending to talk more softly and slowly than the others. They are good listeners, which they may need to be as they are often surrounded by vata and pitta dominated personalities! Kapha types have natural empathy and compassion and are the most loving, loyal and understanding of all the constitutions.

Kapha types work hard, but in a different way to the other two. Vatas and pittas are more self-motivated than kaphas, who love routine and are good at tackling large amounts of work at a steady pace. Vatas need excitement, pittas need to be challenged, but kaphas like stability. In any given task, vatas are good with creative ideas, pittas are good at making them practical and kaphas are good at getting on with doing it.

Kapha people have a strong but slow digestion. They tend to eat bigger meals and then not feel hungry for a long time. They don't need to feel hunger to eat though; they often eat simply because it's dinner time! A kapha person would never forget to eat or want to miss a meal.

The main challenge for kapha constitution is putting on weight, which is difficult to lose. It is like 'a moment on the lips and a lifetime on the hips'. In contrast, pittas can lose weight easily, and vatas can have trouble keeping up their weight.

An indication of an unbalanced kapha constitution can be a lack of motivation, which can lead to depression. In general, pittas and vatas need to relax more, eat well and nurture themselves to stay balanced, whereas kaphas may need the opposite—possibly to eat less (or lighter foods), be more active or take on something more challenging.

Kapha types have natural empathy and compassion and are the most loving, loyal and understanding of all constitutions.

Kapha

How to **unbalance** kapha

- Eat too much heavy food followed by a nice long nap.

- Eat lots of bread, cakes and other comfort foods.

- Lie in late; sleep for more than eight hours.

- Stay indoors and be a couch potato; watch videos back-to-back.

- Follow exactly the same routine every day.

- Procrastinate; assume someone else will do it.

- Never exercise; catch a lift or drive— even for short distances.

- Suppress or deny your feelings.

- Don't speak up; let others take you for granted.

How to **balance** kapha

- Add warming spices like ginger, cardamom or cinnamon to your food and drinks.

- Eat more warm, spicy or naturally bitter foods.

- Have plenty of freshly steamed vegetables.

- Eat wholefoods like brown rice and pulses.

- Get up early; have an energising morning yoga routine.

- Get outside; do some physical activity.

- Make a change; do something different and exciting.

- Declutter your house; finish something you've been putting off.

- Walk or cycle to work.

- Speak up; share your well-considered opinions.

PRAKRITI—BIRTH CONSTITUTION RATIO

We are actually a combination of the three doshas: vata, pitta and kapha. There is a common misconception in Ayurveda that the goal is to become balanced in all three but that's not appropriate for most people. In some people one dosha may dominate, where they exhibit clear traits from one constitution; this is called mono-doshic. In others, two doshas dominate; this is called bi-doshic. If all three are about equal, this is a tri-doshic constitution.

The central concept of Ayurvedic medicine is that our constitution is set at birth, and you remain healthy when your 'birth constitution ratio' (also called prakriti) remains unchanged. Just like our astrological chart, we are all born with a specific constitution ratio. Stress and poor lifestyle can distort our prakriti—and it's this imbalance which can lead to disease. The aim is to keep your prakriti stable throughout life. Prakriti is said to be our optimum setting and when we feel the most 'comfortable in our own skin'.

The actual aim, therefore, is to become a first-rate version of yourself, rather than a second-rate version of someone else. Ayurveda self-knowledge gives you the tools to do this.

KNOW THYSELF

Written in ancient Greek on the Apollo temple in Delphi, the dictum 'know thyself' is also crucial in Ayurvedic healing. An Ayurvedic doctor can check your prakriti from your pulse, or through vedic astrology. Alternatively you can estimate it with questionnaires and checklists.

When you are healthy and well-balanced, you are naturally attracted to the right foods and activities suited to your body type. However, when you are out of balance you will be attracted to the wrong foods and activites which make you worse.

A perfect 'Catch 22' situation!

To halt this downward spiral, an awareness of Ayurveda can help you see what is happening and take the correct actions to return yourself to a position of balance.

BALANCING THE DOSHAS

Vata is a cold constitution so it's important to keep warm and comfortable. Adequate rest and food are essential. Therapies such as Epsom salts baths and massages with warm oils, as well as regular yoga and walks in nature, are very beneficial.

Pitta is a hot constitution so needs to keep cool. These types have a stronger digestion but need to avoid too much rich, spicy food, or excessive coffee and alcohol.

Both vata and pitta types really benefit from 'bringing in the earth element' with regular food and rest and nurturing activities that reduce stress.

Kapha types are just the opposite. They don't tend to get stressed in the same way; they are far too 'laid back'. When kaphas are balanced they are pleasant, reliable and hard-working. When unbalanced, they can put on weight, become lazy and depressed. For them, more of the air and fire elements need to be brought in. Probably a bit less sleep and food will help. This doesn't condemn kaphas to a perpetual boot camp type regime—we are just talking about bringing ourselves back into balance.

Normally kapha types can enjoy their favourite foods, rest and a great sleep. Vatas can enjoy being enthusiastic and moving around. Pittas can enjoy driving their powerful cars and being dynamic.

Keith's One Pot Vata Balance Stew

Warm and nourishing, this stew is suitable for all doshas, particularly for vata in the cooler months.

Serves 4

1 tbsp butter or coconut oil

1 red onion *finely chopped*

1 tsp grated fresh ginger

2 garlic cloves *crushed*

1 tsp of ground paprika

100 g butternut squash *peeled & diced*

1 medium carrot *diced*

50 g red split lentils

350 ml water

1 tsp bouillon stock powder

salt & pepper *to taste*

Sauté the onion, ginger and garlic in the butter/coconut oil until tender. Keep the pan covered and the flame very low so the onions caramelise without burning.

Add the paprika, replace the lid and cook for another minute.

Stir in the carrot and squash, cook on a low heat for 2-3 minutes.

Add the lentils, water and stock powder and bring to the boil. Cover and simmer for 40 minutes, adding more water if it dries out too much.

Add pepper and salt to taste.

The main aim of Ayurveda is to restore and maintain harmony in individuals so they can enjoy and offer their positive qualities to the world. Unfortunately modern life encourages us to rush around, travel and eat at irregular times, all of which upset the delicate balance within us. The good news is that yoga is the best way to balance all the constitution types. In fact it was designed to do just that! A good yoga session will have an activation and relaxation, a variety of postures and forward stretches balanced by backward bends. Yoga creates activity, but also inner stillness.

I've noticed that people who regularly practise yoga naturally start doing the right activities. They eat the correct foods to balance their constitution types, without knowing anything about Ayurveda! The truth is that we all have an inner wisdom that intuitively knows what we need. This gets overridden by stress and cravings. Yoga and a few Ayurvedic principles help you attune to your real needs.

DISCOVER YOURSELF

The following questionnaire will give you a quick guide to estimating your dosha balance. For more accuracy, pulse or facial diagnosis is required.

> Give yourself a score from 1 to 3 where 1 = not at all and 3 = definitely.

> Each page represents a different dosha type.

> Add up your scores on each page. This will give you a score out of 60 for that dosha.

> If your score is around 30, the dosha is average strength, above 40 it is strong and below 25 weak.

Rate yourself
on a scale
of 1 → 3

1 = not at all ··········▶ 3 = definitely

☐ I have a quick mind and grasp new ideas easily.

☐ I forget things very quickly, my short-term memory is best.

☐ My hair tends to be coarse, dry, dark or curly.

☐ I get restless, and like to be on the move doing new exciting things.

☐ I am often in a hurry, rushing from one thing to another.

☐ I tend to be thin and find it difficult to put on weight.

☐ I speak quickly in an enthusiastic and excitable way.

☐ I can be overly sensitive and emotional, and easily feel hurt.

☐ Under stress I tend to become fearful, nervous or worried, sometimes all three.

☐ I am a light sleeper, often waking up early, or have difficulty sleeping generally.

☐ I prefer warm weather and easily feel the cold.

☐ I dislike routine, and enjoy being spontaneous.

☐ I can skip meals or forget to eat.

☐ My digestion is irregular, with gas or bloating.

☐ My feet and hands tend to feel cold.

☐ My skin tends to be thin and dry with prominent veins.

☐ I am very creative, with a good imagination.

☐ I like travelling, art, music, dancing and going out.

☐ I spend money quickly and impulsively.

☐ My joints are thin, protruding, with a tendency to dryness and cracking.

Vata Score

☐

1 = not at all ----------▶ 3 = definitely

☐ I am intelligent with a discriminating and precise mind.

☐ I have a good memory and can recall things clearly and accurately.

☐ My hair is fine and straight, with a tendency to early thinning or greying.

☐ I am purposeful and take pride in my work.

☐ I like to finish a task, and do not like to stop once I have started.

☐ I have a medium build and moderately good physique.

☐ I am concise and clear in my communication.

☐ I am dynamic, strong-willed and can be forceful in nature.

☐ Under stress I can become impatient or angry.

☐ I sleep well and feel rested with 6–7 hours of sleep.

☐ My joints are moderately strong, loose and flexible.

☐ I usually feel warm, but sometimes hot and bothered. I prefer cooler weather.

☐ I am task-orientated and tend to be competitive.

☐ I have a good appetite and can eat a large meal if I want to.

☐ I have a tendency to get acid indigestion or heartburn.

☐ During activity I get hot, thirsty and perspire easily.

☐ My skin is warm and reddish and prone to sunburn.

☐ I am technically-minded and can find solutions to problems.

☐ I like sports, keeping fit, debates or politics.

☐ I like to look good and spend money on luxuries.

Pitta Score

☐

1 = not at all ----------► 3 = definitely

☐ I tend to learn things slowly but surely.

☐ Once I have learnt something, I tend to remember it for a long time.

☐ My hair tends to be abundant, thick and wavy.

☐ I am easy-going and happy to support others.

☐ I prefer to work at a steady and comfortable pace.

☐ I have a heavy build and can easily put on weight, which is difficult to lose again.

☐ I am a good listener, and sensitive to others.

☐ I tend to be forgiving and kind-natured.

☐ I deal with stress by withdrawing or walking away.

☐ I sleep deeply and need at least 8 hours a night.

☐ I like warm weather or to wrap up by the fire.

☐ I like routine and I don't like change.

☐ I have a tendency to overeat and may feel heavy or tired after a meal.

☐ I am prone to get nasal congestion and blocked up with excess mucus.

☐ My hands are cool and normally moist.

☐ My skin is cool but thick and smooth.

☐ I am methodical, steady and business minded.

☐ I like gardening, staying at home or cooking.

☐ I like to save money and make things last.

☐ My joints are strong, large and well formed.

Kapha Score

☐

My
Favourite
Ingredients

Food is a reflection of humanity's relationship with nature. From the very first cultivated vegetables, grains and pulses to the massive variety of foods we enjoy today, food is living history on a plate.

The first cultivated foods in Europe and the Middle East were wheat, chick peas, lentils and linseeds. In China it was millet and rice, in America early crops were corn, beans and squash.

Here's a brief overview of the ingredients I've come to love cooking with over the years.

GRAINS

I consider grains to be the mother of all foods. The Isle of Anglesey, where I live, is affectionately called Mam Cymru, literally meaning 'Mother of Wales'. Historically, lots of wheat was grown in its flat, fertile fields to provide the daily bread for the whole area.

Grains, with their energy-giving carbohydrate and body-building fats and proteins, are a food worthy of the gods! In many cultures, grains are literally worshipped for their life-giving qualities and are the basis of most meals in cultures all over the world.

I generally like to use wholegrains such as short grain brown rice or millet. They are a slow-release carbohydrate and contain more nutrients and protein than refined products. Within a whole grain, nature has provided all the phytonutrients (natural compounds such as digestive enzymes) that you need to absorb its nutrients. In vegetarian cooking, grains combined with pulses are the easiest source of protein.

RICE is the most consumed grain in the world, being the main staple food in Asia. In China it has been cultivated for over 10,000 years.

Rice is held sacred by many communities. In India it is dyed with turmeric and used as an offering for religious ceremonies. Indeed in South India it is called Anna Laxmi. 'Anna' is the Sanskrit word for food and 'Laxmi' is the goddess of wealth. Rice there is symbolic of abundance, both in food and wealth.

In the West, since Roman times, wheat grain was thrown at weddings to symbolise wealth and fertility. This tradition continued in Europe but was later replaced by white rice (which conveniently matched the colour scheme of a wedding).

Although potatoes have taken over as a staple carbohydrate since then, thankfully the idea of throwing them at weddings has not caught on yet.

SHORT GRAIN BROWN RICE is an everyday ingredient for me. I normally start cooking with the brown rice and pulses, and prepare the rest of the meal as they are cooking. In Macrobiotic food, rice is normally slightly overcooked and sticky which makes it sweeter and easier to digest. For some dishes I also like rice just cooked so it is still slightly nutty, with the grains staying separate. It is recommended that you chew it slowly and notice the flavours change in your mouth. The digestive process begins in the mouth, and you can notice the flavour becoming sweeter as the carbohydrate is broken down to sugars.

RISOTTO RICE is much more starchy than long grain rice and goes sticky when it is cooked. I discovered its merits quite by accident when making kitcheri. I was about to do a cookery demonstration in a workshop in Australia, but forgot to buy any basmati rice. A hurried search through the cupboards rewarded us with a packet of risotto rice. So I used it instead, and to my relief it was a complete success. I pretended that it was my intention all along!

BASMATI RICE Indian people are as passionate about their rice as the French are about their cheese and the British are about their tea. The equivalent of a fine Brie cheese or best Yorkshire tea, basmati rice is considered one of the best. And just as in dog breeding, the pedigree makes a difference to the quality and price. Most of the best basmati is grown in Pakistan and the north western parts of India.

Compared with other types of rice, basmati is particularly elegant, with its long and slender grains. As it cooks it gets even more beautiful as it elongates further. Truly a rice of breeding, basmati stays discreetly separate, each grain holding its shape during cooking.

It not only looks good, but smells good too. Basmati literally means 'fragrant rice' as it gives off a pleasant aroma when cooked. In India a herb called padan gives off a similar aroma. You'll be shocked to learn that some people cheat by cooking cheaper rice with padan leaves and then pass it off as basmati! Don't worry though, this adulteration is unlikely to happen in Britain where the herb is more expensive to buy than the rice.

QUINOA, pronounced 'keen wah', is a small millet-like seed which thinks it's a grain!

It was first cultivated about 5,000 years ago in the mountains of Peru. There is a beautiful legend that a sacred bird known as 'Kullku' brought the first quinoa seeds in its little beak as a gift from the gods.

Quinoa was subsequently revered greatly, because it would grow at great altitudes and was extremely nutritious. Quinoa was called the 'mother grain' by the Inca people. Not only did it allow the population to thrive in their mountain environment but it also had spiritual qualities. It was even found to deepen meditation.

Unlike grains, quinoa is a complete protein. It also has twice the amount of calcium as grains, is high in potassium, other minerals and B vitamins.

Quinoa helps normalise the acid/alkaline balance in the body. Whereas most grains are acid-forming in the body, quinoa helps promote a healthy alkaline environment.

MILLET is one of the world's most important grains and sustains one-third of the world's population. Its cultivation dates back over 5,000 years. It can tolerate hot or cold environments and is a very fast-growing grain—harvested within 2 months of planting. Its ability to grow on poor soils with little water means it is widely used in Africa, Russia and China.

Even though we get more than our fair share of rain in Wales, we still like to use millet! It is a small grain which I often dry-roast before boiling in stock, then allow it to absorb most of the water. It cooks quickly. I like to cook it until the grains are still separate, giving it a slightly nutty texture.

Millet has an alkalising effect, so it can help to correct the acid/alkaline balance in the body. It also has a strong antifungal action, so it can help reduce candida overgrowth and encourage healthy gut bacteria. Millet is rich in potassium and magnesium, and has a high silicon content. It's a shame we don't eat more millet in our Western diets, instead of just feeding it to budgerigars!

OATS are a fantastic grain that thrive in cooler climates and poorer soils. It's a unique food that relaxes the nerves and strengthens the body. Oat straw is actually a recognised herbal remedy to soothe nervous tension. The grain contains a lot of soluble fibre which slows down the release of carbohydrates. This means that eating oats in the morning can keep you going right up to lunchtime.

Traditionally oats were a Scottish favourite in savoury dishes like soups and haggis, as well as in baking and breads. With a high content of iron, zinc and magnesium, oats deserve their reputation for strength-giving qualities loved by burly Scotsmen everywhere as their favourite breakfast.

I like to have my oats too! First thing in the morning, my perfect breakfast is soaked oats with fruit and yoghurt. In winter I have hot porridge with honey and tahini.

Muesli was a health breakfast devised by Dr Bircher-Benner in Switzerland. It was inspired by a traditional dish in the Alps.

The original Bircher-Benner muesli recipe has far more fruit and nuts than grains.

Bircher-Benner Style Muesli

Soaking the oats makes them more digestible. The other ingredients are added just before serving.

40 g whole almonds

2 tbsp rolled oats

1 tbsp goji berries

100 ml water or apple juice

1 apple

½ lemon *juiced*

2 tbsp kefir or single cream

1 tsp raw honey

¼ tsp ground cinnamon

The night before Grind the almonds with a pestle and mortar or an electric grinder. Soak the ground almonds, oats and berries in the water and leave overnight.

In the morning Grate the apple into a bowl and add the lemon juice. Add the soaked ingredients. Stir in the kefir/cream, honey and cinnamon. Serve immediately.

CORN As wheat and rice were cultivated in Europe and Asia, corn (or maize) was the grain cultivated in America. Before European contact, corn was the staple food of the Aztec Indians, who revered maize. Centeotl was their corn god, depicted as a handsome young man with a yellow complexion and a headdress decorated with maize. He holds a bowl, perhaps anticipating the arrival of corn flakes?

Corn flakes were invented by Dr John Kellogg over 125 years ago. He was a doctor and naturopath, and actually ran a health sanatorium where people enjoyed healthy food, exercise and therapies. Corn flakes were initially intended as a healthy, gluten-free alternative to the normal breakfast at the time—eggs and meat. Dr Kellogg further transformed our morning meal by inventing and popularising peanut butter.

Sugar was later added to the cereal against his wishes, and then of course came the invention of the peanut butter (and jam) toastie!

You can use sweetcorn to add colour and flavour to meals. I use the organic product as much as possible and try to avoid genetically modified corn.

WHEAT has been cultivated for at least 10,000 years. Its use in the Middle East allowed city cultures to develop and encouraged the spread of civilisation. It was easy to store, could be eaten as a grain or ground up to make bread, one of the world's first 'ready meals'. Wheat is also higher in protein than most grains.

Wheat grains were not only used to shower the bride with at weddings, people also made the bridal bouquet from stalks of wheat.

In Greek mythology Demeter was the goddess of agriculture, and her sacred symbol was the ears of wheat. Her daughter, Persephone, was abducted by Hades and held captive in the underworld. During Demeter's frantic search for her lost daughter, no crops would grow and the world entered into a perpetual winter.

Eventually Zeus himself declared that Persephone should be released, but could only return to her mother if she had not eaten any food. As fate would have it she had eaten six pomegranate seeds! Zeus then decreed that for each seed she had eaten, she must spend that number of months each year with Hades and the other six months with Demeter. This was how the seasons were created. Every year, heralded by the warm south wind, Persephone returns to Demeter, the goddess of vegetation, who then resumes her duties and brings forth the spring.

So much of our culture and history are connected to this grain, it's ironic that a lot of people have now become sensitive or allergic to wheat products. This may be because wheat has been genetically modified so much over the years.

Spelt flour is more like the original wheat grown hundreds of years ago. It makes bread and cakes a bit heavier because it contains less gluten.

Sometimes it's not so much the wheat, but the yeast in bread that doesn't agree with people. This can disturb the natural microbes in the digestive tract. I prefer a good-quality sourdough bread with natural yeasts and bacteria. They produce lactic acid which makes the bread sour and more digestible. A good sourdough has gut-friendly bacteria.

Wheat can be eaten like rice as a grain, and this avoids the yeast problem. It is also great sprouted. The sprouting actually breaks down the gluten and makes the grain sweeter.

Young shoots of wheatgrass can be juiced to make wheatgrass juice packed with chlorophyll, enzymes and nutrients.

If you have a serious gluten allergy you have to avoid wheat, and also barley, rye and oats which are related to wheat and contain gluten.

KAMUT WHEAT Like spelt, kamut is a very old strain of wheat with the most interesting story of all.

After the Second World War, an American airman was based in Egypt in 1947. During his adventures he found some wheat grains that had lain hidden in an ancient Pharaoh's tomb for 4,000 years. He passed 36 of these precious seeds to a fellow airman, Earl Dedman, who sent them to his family in Montana.

The Dedman family planted the grains. 32 of the seeds germinated and grew into healthy wheat plants. They first called it 'King Tuts Wheat' after the Egyptian Pharaoh, and later it became 'kamut wheat'. They then grew the kamut in small plots, and it turned into a proper pyramid selling scheme. It was also called the mummy of all grains.

Between 1950 and 1965 kamut was grown as a novelty, but by 1975 the interest had worn off and the wheat was nearly forgotten again. But this grain had a destiny. It hadn't waited 4,000 years and travelled 7,000 miles for nothing!

In 1977 Bob Quinn remembered the legendary wheat, and set out to find some. After a long search he managed to find just one precious jar. His father turned this into 40 kilos of grain, growing it in his back garden.

In 1985 the wheat was successfully introduced to the health food market, and the rest is history. Now there are over 45,000 acres of kamut wheat in North America alone.

Kamut has a larger grain and contains more protein and antioxidants than normal wheat. It's also richer in magnesium, zinc and selenium, and has up to 30% more vitamin E. It's a high-energy grain as it has a high percentage of lipids, which provide more energy than carbohydrates.

Perhaps the greatest treasure in the pyramids was not the gold itself, but the golden seeds that time forgot.

BARLEY, like wheat, is a staple grain throughout Europe and Asia, though it's also revered for providing a vital pillar of Western civilisation ... beer! For a while I lived near a brewery, and a few days a week a delicious, sweet aroma used to fill the air. It was the barley being malted. Malting allows the grain to sprout so the enzymes convert the starch into sugar (maltose). Then the grain is air-dried to stop the germination, and the malt is extracted from the grain and used for brewing.

Barley is also used to make malted drinks like Horlicks, sweets like Maltesers, and caffeine-free coffee substitutes.

Before potatoes became widely used, barley was the staple food of the masses. It was cheaper than wheat, which was more of a rich man's grain. Barley will grow in colder climates than wheat, so is more popular in areas like Tibet, Russia and Eastern Europe.

Barley flat bread is a yeast-free rustic flat bread made with baking soda. Barley is heavier than wheat, so expect a cross between a soda bread and a biscuit. It's quick and easy to make because it doesn't need to rise.

Olde Barley Flat Bread

200 g barley flour

½ tsp bicarbonate of soda

½ tsp salt

200 ml buttermilk or live yoghurt

10 g butter

Makes 6 slices

Heat the oven to 180°C. Lightly grease a baking tray. Sift the flour, bicarb and salt into a mixing bowl. Rub the butter into the flour. Add enough buttermilk/yoghurt to form a dough.

Turn the dough out onto a lightly floured surface, and use your hands to form it into a round, flat shape about 1 cm thick. Slide the loaf onto the baking tray. Use a knife to score the top of the loaf to mark the slices. Using a fork, make indentations over the top of the loaf.

Bake until light golden in colour, about 25 minutes. Cut or break into wedges along the score lines and serve hot.

Keith's Summer Barley Water

200 g organic pearl barley

1¼ litres water

juice of 1 lemon

1 tbsp honey

5 cardamom pods

1 cm cinnamon stick

1 tbsp grated fresh ginger

Makes 3 to 4 glasses

Rinse, wash and drain the barley.
Place in a medium saucepan.
Add the water, cinnamon,
cardamom and ginger.

Bring to the boil and simmer for 20
minutes. Don't let it dry out. You should
be left with about half the liquid.
Top up if necessary. Allow to cool.

Strain the water into a jug.
Add the lemon juice and honey.
Chill and serve.

BARLEY WATER Barley can be used to make a refreshing cool drink: barley water. When I grew up there were three cold drinks that we were allowed to have: water, orange squash or lemon barley water.

It was no accident that barley water became a popular summer drink. It's very refreshing and actually has a cooling effect on the body. It's slightly thicker than water so it rehydrates and quenches your thirst more effectively than pure water.

Barley water can act as an antibiotic for very mild infections. When lemon is added it becomes an excellent tonic for your kidneys. It's also high in vitamins and minerals. It's a good diuretic and so helps to flush toxins out of your system. So as well as being nourishing and refreshing, this drink helps to detoxify your urinary tract and therefore discourages UTI (urinary tract infections).

PEARL BARLEY The barley is polished to remove the bran and husk from the grain to make it softer and quicker to cook. Its main use is in stews and soups, and it's a key ingredient in Scotch broth.

Ayurvedic Scotch Broth

You may not think of Scotch broth as a typical Ayurvedic dish—but to me it is! That's because it is made with the seasonal and local ingredients that are perfectly suited to the climate here in Wales and Scotland. The barley, peas and vegetables are really nourishing during the long winters in this part of the world. This recipe makes a large pan full, so halve the quantity for one or two people.

Serves 4

1 tbsp butter or coconut oil

250 g potatoes *peeled & diced*

250 g swedes *peeled & diced*

2 onions *peeled & sliced*

1 celery stick *sliced*

1 leek *sliced*

2½ ltrs vegetable stock

100 g pearl barley *rinsed*

100 g green split peas

75 g kale *finely chopped*

salt & pepper *to taste*

Melt the butter/coconut oil and sauté all vegetables, except for the kale, in a large saucepan for 2–3 minutes.

Add the vegetable stock, washed barley and split peas.

Cover with a lid, bring to the boil and simmer gently for 60 minutes or until the peas and pearl barley are soft.

Stir in the kale and cook for a further 15 minutes, or until all the ingredients are well cooked.

Season to taste with salt and pepper.

POTATO isn't a grain, of course, but where I grew up in the UK it's used instead of rice or bread in a meal as a source of carbohydrate. I love potatoes as they're my comfort food, or mother's food. They are similar in composition to cooked grains, being mostly carbohydrate with a small amount of protein.

Originally from South America, where they have about 3,000 varieties, the potato came to Europe with the Spanish in the 16th century. The typical spud we know and love today was probably developed and refined by growers in the Canary Isles.

The potato was viewed with suspicion at first as it is related to deadly nightshade. In fact it is only the underground parts of the plant that are actually edible. Even now Macrobiotic and Ayurvedic cooking do not generally recommend potatoes, because they are regarded as slightly toxic. The toxicity of the raw potato increases if it sprouts or goes green. (Although the 'eyes' help them to see you through the week.)

Their big advantage is that they produce a high yield of sustaining food. Yields in the UK are about seven tonnes per hectare for grains and forty tonnes for potatoes! Grains increase their weight when cooked but potatoes rovide 2–3 times more food. Their widespread availability contributed to the increase in European populations. Production really took off in the 1700s, with potatoes as the 'food fuel' of the industrial revolution.

From Europe, settlers took the potato all the way back across the Atlantic Ocean to North America, although wild varieties already grew there. Later they returned to Europe, this time as 'American fries'.

I love my traditional potato dishes— mashed, roasted and new with butter. Spicy Indian recipes are delicious and I particularly like the South Indian dosa with potato filling.

Nutritionally potatoes are probably most similar to white rice or white bread, having fewer nutrients and a higher glycaemic index (GI) than whole grains. The carbohydrate in potatoes is converted to sugar quite quickly. Whole grains have the advantage that the carbs are released more slowly and contain more nutrients. I find a meal with whole grains is more filling and satisfies longer than a potato-based meal.

BARLEY GRASS

We all know that the grass is greener on the other side. But why is it greener? It's due to a magic molecule called chlorophyll which is bright green. It uses the sunlight to convert carbon dioxide and water into simple carbohydrates.

Young barley leaves are full of this chlorophyll which has a very similar molecular structure to haemoglobin in our own blood. The big difference is that chlorophyll has magnesium as its central atom and haemoglobin has iron. So whenever I drink barley grass juice I almost feel like I'm having a blood transfusion! Barley grass juice is the closest we get to liquid sunshine—the energy of the sun captured and made into food.

Good farmers know that sweet young grass is the best food for their animals. The only problem is digesting this nourishing but tough little plant. Cows have developed four stomach compartments to do it, but we only have one! A vegetable juicer can act like a substitute first stomach for us, extracting the nutritious juice from the indigestible fibre.

FRESH OR DRIED BARLEY GRASS?

You can have your own fresh barley grass juice if you have the right sort of juicer or if you live near a good juice bar. A mere 30 ml of fresh juice is equivalent in nutritional value to a kilogram of leafy green vegetables. Barley grass juice has more vitamin C than oranges and twice as much vitamin A as carrots.

Fresh juice has the advantage of being a truly living food with all the enzymes fully active. You can buy trays of ready-to-use barley or wheat grass, or grow your own in seed trays. You will need a masticating juicer to extract the juice as the grass needs to be crushed to release the juice. A normal centrifugal juicer will not extract it very well.

Otherwise the more concentrated dried juice powder is a great substitute. It is much more convenient and easy to source. You can take it with you to have some during the day and there is no washing up.

Just one teaspoon of barley grass powder is equivalent to an entire bowl of spinach. In a crisis Popeye would have found a tub of barley grass powder much more practical than tins of spinach!

Fresh or dried, barley grass is a true superfood. It contains a full spectrum of vitamins and minerals, including calcium, phosphorus, magnesium, sodium and potassium, all in a well-balanced ratio. It is also a complete source of protein, supplying all the essential amino acids.

Barley grass has many essential enzymes, including protease that assists in protein digestion, lipase (a fat-splitting enzyme) and transhydrogenase which strengthens the heart muscles.

It is also noted for having a high concentration of superoxide dismutase (SOD) enzyme which breaks down free radicals in the body. So, in addition to flooding the body with nutrients, barley grass is a powerful detoxifier. The beneficial enzymes help neutralise and remove toxins and environmental pollutants from the body.

Barley grass is often considered to be gluten-free because it's cut before the grain forms. People who are intolerant to gluten and barley grains can normally take the juice.

Barley grass is packed full of nutrients and it is a powerful detoxifier.

PULSES

If grains are like the mother of all foods, then pulses must be the father—the perfect marriage! Both pulses and grains are 'incomplete proteins', meaning they are each deficient in certain amino acids. However, together they compensate for each other's shortcomings because the grains contain the amino acids missing in the pulses and vice versa. Cooked together as in kitcheri their qualities are even more closely entwined and beneficial. Rice has an enzyme that actually helps break down the starch in pulses. Most of my meals are based on a combination of these two foods.

People tend to be a bit afraid of the digestive wind-forming qualities of pulses. To help counteract this we use a lot of split pulses like lentils, which are easier to cook. We cook them for a long time which really breaks down the indigestible starches and makes them taste sweeter. Many of the spices we use in the recipes also aid digestion, particularly asafoetida which is commonly used in Indian dhal (lentil dish).

I also use whole beans. These are excellent nutritionally, but do need to be soaked and rinsed well. A good pressure cooker reduces the cooking time of pre-soaked beans by two-thirds.

BROWN LENTILS

These are whole red lentils with the brown skin still on. Being whole, they take longer to cook and are a bit more nutty. They do not dissolve when cooked like red lentils but remain more intact. I use them in richer stews and for sprouting. Once the sprout is longer than the original seed you can eat it raw as a high-vitality snack. Green lentils are larger and can be used in the same way.

YELLOW/GREEN SPLIT PEAS

Split peas are my real favourite. They take a bit longer to cook than lentils and benefit from soaking, but they have a delicious flavour of their own. They are hearty, substantial and economical. Like red lentils they really melt away as you cook them, so are a perfect filler for soups and stews and can also be formed into bakes or rissoles. The bright yellow peas are a good colour and blend well with most vegetables.

Related to garden peas, split peas were one of the first cultivated foods in Europe and a major food during the Middle Ages.

RED LENTILS

The humble lentil is perhaps the most underestimated of all foods. Quick, easy to cook and high in protein, it can provide hidden nourishment in many dishes. It does not have a strong flavour of its own, so it is an ideal base for vegetable stews and soups. Lentil soup (dhal) eaten with chappatis is the basis of a lot of traditional meals in India. Sometimes it is cooked together with rice to make kitcheri. Cooked lentils can also be baked to form a high-protein savoury loaf.

The shape of a camera lens is basically the same shape as a lentil. 'Lens' is the original Latin name for lentil. So it could explain why vegetarian cookbooks are so focused on using lentils.

Lentils were one of the earliest known cultivated crops. In the biblical story, Esau, the elder brother of Jacob, had been working in the field and was faint with hunger. Jacob had prepared a wonderful lentil and vegetable soup and Esau asked his brother for a helping (mess of pottage). Jacob offered to exchange it in return for Esau's inheritance. Esau was so hungry he agreed. 'Mess of pottage' is a phrase now used to describe this foolish selling off of something precious, but of future value, for the sake of instant gratification. Eating unhealthy food is just like that mess of pottage. We eat the food that seems immediately gratifying, but in the process we sell off our inheritance of good health.

KIDNEY BEANS Another great food originating in South America, kidney beans are delicious, easy-to-use and have the benefit of adding colour to a meal. Raw kidney beans are toxic and they must be soaked overnight and properly cooked for at least 60 minutes. They should not be sprouted or eaten raw. Once cooked properly they are a great filler for wraps and spicy dishes. They are also good mixed with other cooked beans to make colourful salads.

SPLIT MUNG BEANS These are popular in Indian cooking and are available in Asian grocery shops. Shelled split mung beans look a bit like yellow lentils and can be used in the same way. Some have the shells still on, which adds a bit more texture and flavour. Split mung beans and white basmati rice are the main ingredients of kitcheri.

MUNG BEANS These small, whole green beans need more cooking than split pulses but because of their size they cook relatively quickly. They can be soaked overnight to reduce the cooking time. They are best cooked until they begin to break up a bit as this improves the flavour. This will take about an hour. Like split peas, mung beans have their own delicious flavour. When cooked properly they are soft and very easy on your digestive system.

Wild mung beans are thought to have originated in Mongolia (or Mungolia), but the main area of cultivation is in India, where they have been a popular crop for over 4,000 years. From there, they spread to China and other parts of Asia and Africa. I make a special kitcheri from whole mung beans. First I soak the mung beans overnight, and then cook them together with short grain brown rice and bouillon powder (page 314). Mung beans are also great sprouted.

Sprouting Mung Beans

Organic mung beans tend to sprout faster than non-organic. Professional sprouter kits can be purchased but you can also use a small bowl and some muslin cloth.

Wash the mung beans. Place them in twice their volume of water and soak overnight.

Drain and wash them in cold water. Cover with the muslin cloth and leave in a warm place out of direct sunlight, perhaps in a cupboard.

Rinse them 2 or 3 times a day to moisten. The sprouts should be ready to eat in a couple of days, once the shoots are longer than the beans.

The young shoots are nutty and crunchy, and are a great source of protein. The process of germination breaks down the starches in the seeds, making them digestible without having to be cooked. You'll find sprouted mung beans are used a lot in Chinese cooking, often in stir fried dishes.

BUTTER BEANS Although popular in Greek and European cooking, these beans actually originated in South America. They are also called Lima beans, as they were exported from Lima in Peru. Succotash, a traditional Native American dish that combines this delicious bean with corn, became popular in the US depression of the 1930s served as a stew or hearty pie. "Sufferin' succotash" is a phrase used by the Looney Tunes cartoon character Sylvester the cat, often during another foiled attempt to catch Tweety the bird.

These larger beans definitely need soaking overnight and cooking for at least an hour, or 20 minutes in a pressure cooker. Exact cooking times depend on how old the beans are—older ones take longer to cook. Soaking is important because it starts the process of germination and helps make all beans more digestible. Butter beans have a delicious buttery flavour and are versatile in soups and stews.

Ideally, I prefer to use dried beans which are cheaper and more nutritious than tinned. However, I sometimes do use the latter for convenience.

Succotash

This is based on a Native American Indian staple dish. It is quite simple but surprisingly satisfying. You can really tell how the corn and beans complement each other, and it's far more nourishing than eating corn or beans on their own. You can of course use fresh corn for this dish. Steam or boil a fresh cob of corn until tender. When cool enough to handle, carefully cut the kernels from the husk and add to the dish.

Serves 4

2 tbsp butter

1 garlic clove *finely chopped*

1 small onion *diced*

1 medium red pepper *diced*

1 medium courgette *diced*

400 g tin of butter beans *drained*

250 g tin organic sweetcorn kernels *drained*

2 tsp chopped fresh sage

1 tsp chopped fresh thyme

salt & pepper *to taste*

Slowly melt the butter in a large pan.

Add the garlic and onion. Cover and cook gently until translucent, about 10 minutes.

Add the pepper and courgette, season with salt and pepper. Cook for another 10 minutes, stirring occasionally, until the vegetables are tender.

Add the corn and butter beans.

Cook for a further 5 minutes.

Stir in the herbs and serve.

ADZUKI BEANS look similar to mung beans but are red in colour. They can be cooked from raw but are much better soaked first. They are popular in Macrobiotic cooking, add a rich red colour to a meal, and are thought to be therapeutic for the kidneys.

Adzuki beans originated in East Asia and are particularly popular in Japan. Their name comes from the Japanese 'small bean', as opposed to soya which means 'large bean'. In Japanese cooking they are used in red bean paste and sweet dishes. Such is the Japanese love for the adzuki that Pepsi even launched an adzuki-flavoured cola drink!

In Wales, adzuki are also called red dragon beans. So it's no surprise that we named our adzuki pie 'Welsh Red Dragon Pie'.

Welsh Red Dragon Pie

This is a hearty, meat-free version of shepherd's pie.
It's inexpensive, colourful and delicious. What could be better?

Serves 4-6

100 g adzuki beans

600 ml stock

3 tbsp butter

1 onion *peeled & finely chopped*

1 clove garlic *peeled & finely chopped*

225 g carrots *diced*

1 tbsp tamari

2 tbsp tomato puree

1 tsp mixed herbs

900 g potatoes *peeled & diced*

3 tbsp milk

3 tbsp double cream

salt & pepper *to taste*

Place the beans in the stock and bring to the boil.

Cover with a lid and simmer for 50 minutes.

Meanwhile melt half the butter in a large pan and fry the onion and garlic gently for 5 minutes. Add the carrots and cook for a further 3 minutes.

Pour the cooked adzuki bean mixture over the carrots.

Mix in the tamari, tomato puree and herbs.

Simmer for another 20 minutes so that all the flavours are well blended. Top up with a little more water if it dries out too much. By the end of the cooking, the beans should be breaking up and forming a thick rich stew.

Meanwhile, preheat the oven to 180°C. Steam the potatoes until soft and tender. Mash them with the milk, double cream and remaining butter. Season both the bean mixture and the potatoes to taste.

Put the bean mixture into a 20 cm casserole dish, spread the mashed potatoes on top. Bake for 20 minutes or until the potatoes are crisp and brown.

CHICK PEAS Whether cooked fresh or straight out of a tin, chick peas are a great addition to any meal. In Europe chick peas are the basis of hearty soups and dips such as hummus. They also make great bean sprouts, which can be eaten raw.

Chick peas have been cultivated for thousands of years in Asia and the Middle East. They were a popular food in Ancient Egypt, Greece and Rome. The ones grown in India are smaller and are a staple food. Popular as a protein-rich food they are used in savoury dishes, or dried and salted as a snack.

Chick pea flour, known as 'gram' flour, is also popular in Indian cooking. It is used to make an egg-free batter to coat vegetables which are then fried, or to make a savoury omelette. It is also an ingredient in Indian confectionery, particularly the laddhu (a round sweet).

The popular Hindu god, Ganesh, is often depicted holding a round laddhu ball.

One day all the gods went to visit Shiva and Parvati, the parents of Ganesh and his brother Kartik. They came with the gift of a special laddhu made with sacred ingredients.

Both of the boys wanted this fabulous sweet, so their parents set them a challenge. The first one to travel around the world would win the prize.

Immediately Kartik flew off at great speed on his trusted steed, a peacock. Ganesh was less mobile, being an elephant and having only a small rat as his vehicle!

Instead of trying to dash off, he began to walk respectfully around his parents.

This he did three times.

Extremely puzzled, Shiva asked Ganesh why he wasn't taking up the challenge to travel round the world. Ganesh replied that he had already done so—by walking round his parents. 'You are my world,' he said.

Parvati and Shiva were so pleased by his answer they rewarded him with the laddhu.

Kartik and the peacock returned, exhausted, only to find they had already lost!

Luckily, you only need to travel as far as your kitchen to make this simple recipe.

Ganesh's Favourite Laddhus

250 g gram flour

125 g grated jaggery

100 g ghee

1 tsp ground cardamom

Makes 6 laddhus

Using a non-stick pan, dry roast the flour on a medium heat for 5–10 minutes until it smells roasted. Stir continuously to prevent burning.

Add the ghee and melt it into the flour.

Cook for a further 3 minutes, then remove from the heat.

Add the jaggery and cardamom and stir well until all the ingredients are thoroughly combined.

As the mixture cools, shape into balls.

NUTS & SEEDS

If grains and pulses are the mother and father of vegetarian food, then nuts and seeds must be the friendly uncles and aunts. They are the most 'meaty' of vegetarian foods being high in protein and fat. Ideally, you can combine grains, pulses and nuts/seeds to create complete proteins. Use mostly grains, some pulses and a sprinkle of nuts and seeds.

Nuts and seeds are high in essential fatty acids. Pumpkin seeds, linseeds, chia seeds and walnuts have a high ratio of omega-3 (see 'My favourite fats and oils' page 209).

SUNFLOWER SEEDS I think sunflower seeds are totally underrated. The plants have a magical quality. They are as tall as a person and the flower heads actually turn to follow the sun throughout the day.

The sunflower was revered by the Aztecs, who worshipped the sun god, Inti. The priestesses would wear sunflowers as their sacred headdress. There is also a Greek legend that a water nymph, Clyte, fell in love with the handsome sun god, Apollo. Each day she would stand by the side of her favourite pool and gaze at him as he crossed the sky in his golden chariot drawn by divine white horses. She continued her silent vigil day after day. After some time her feet began to take root and her outstretched hands offered in supplication turned into leaves. Her face became the beautiful sunflower which, to this day, silently follows the course of her secret love, the brilliant sun.

It was a tragic tale because her unconditional love was unrequited. Clyte loved Apollo who was in love with Daphne, who did not return his love. So everyone lost out in the end. Apart from us, as we have the sunflower.

Sunflower seeds are delicious roasted and can be ground up to make toppings or desserts. I use sunflower seeds in my nut roast and sometimes toast them with tamari to make a delicious snack. They can also be sprouted as a nutritious raw food snack.

SUNFLOWER & THE THREE SISTERS

The Native Americans planted the 'three sisters' as companion plants: corn, climbing beans and squash.

The corn provided a stem for the bean plant to climb up. The climbing beans fixed nitrogen to the soil and fertilised it. And the squash provided ground cover to suppress weeds while its prickles discouraged pests. In dietary terms they are a perfect combination too as they provide a balanced meal with complete protein.

Sunflowers were sometimes planted along with the corn, beans and squash, and were known as the fourth sister.

PUMPKIN SEEDS Pumpkins, a type of squash, have been cultivated in the Americas since ancient times.

The pumpkin seed, like the hemp seed, is high in good-quality protein. Both are also high in iron, zinc, magnesium and omega-3 essential fatty acids.

Herbal medicine regards pumpkin seeds as an important parasitic worm remedy. Pumpkin seeds also have a balancing effect on the prostate gland.

Pumpkins are, of course, synonymous with Halloween, which was originally known as 'All Hallows' Eve' (the day before All Hallows' Day, or All Saints' Day). It comes from an ancient Celtic ritual on 31st October, the end of the harvest and beginning of winter. It is believed to be one of the times when the boundaries between the physical and spirit worlds become blurred, so spirits can cross the boundary and create mischief.

If you can't beat them, join them. This led to the dressing up as witches and such like.

The Halloween lantern tradition symbolises Jack O' Lantern, one of those spirits who sold his soul to the devil on the condition that he wouldn't go to hell. Unfortunately, he was not allowed into heaven either! So he's said to still roam the earth with his trademark lamp.

Originally the lanterns were made from turnips and then swedes, but these were hard to cut and make into a lantern face. Immigrants to the USA found pumpkins much bigger and easier to cut and hollow out, and started using them instead.

A type of loaf, Barm Brack, is part of the Irish Halloween custom. It traditionally contained various objects baked into the bread as a sort of fortune-telling game—often a medallion, a stick, a piece of cloth, a small coin or a ring. These, when received in a slice, conveyed a special meaning: the medallion foretold a special blessing; the stick, disputes to be resolved; the cloth meant bad luck; the coin, good fortune; and the ring would indicate marriage.

Barm Brack

There's nothing like the aroma of freshly baked bread filling your kitchen. This is like a sliced tea cake that you can enjoy with a nice cup of Ayurvedic tea.

220 g dried mixed fruit

400 ml apple juice

60 ml warm milk

2 tsp active dry yeast

2 tsp grated jaggery or coconut sugar

300 g wholemeal flour

2 tbsp maple syrup

½ tsp ground cinnamon

½ tsp ground mixed spice

1 large egg *beaten*

75 g unsalted butter

½ tsp salt

Soak the dried fruit in the apple juice overnight.

Mix together the warm milk, yeast and syrup and set aside for 5 minutes to activate the yeast.

Sift the flour into a large bowl. Add the salt and spices. Rub the butter and jaggery/coconut sugar into the flour mix. Make a well in the centre and pour in the beaten egg and the yeast mixture. Stir with a wooden spoon to form a dough. Add more milk if it's too dry or more flour if too moist. Knead for 5–10 minutes on a floured board until the dough is smooth.

Drain the fruit and knead it into the dough a little at a time. Place the dough in a bowl, cover with a tea towel. Leave to rise for 1–1½ hours. It may take longer depending on the temperature of the room. Once it's doubled in size, knead it again for another couple of minutes. Place in a lightly buttered medium-sized cake tin. Cover again and leave to rise in a warm place for a further 45–90 minutes until it has doubled in size.

Meanwhile, preheat the oven to 180°C. Bake the Barm Brack for 25–35 minutes until browned.

SESAME SEEDS Sesame is thought to be the oldest cultivated seed. It has a very high oil content and can grow in arid conditions. As long as there is water for germination it can grow where other crops fail. It is very popular in Asia and the Middle East.

The small but mighty sesame seed can turn the simplest of dishes into a meal. Simple vegetable dishes are transformed with a sprinkling of roasted sesame seeds. Even McDonalds have caught on and use them on their bread. Nearly the entire sesame crop from Mexico is used to garnish burger buns in the USA!

Roasted, ground and mixed with salt, the seeds make Gomasio (page 182), a Macrobiotic condiment that can be used instead of table salt.

Ground sesame seeds also become the wonderful tahini—a delicious protein-rich paste so versatile that you can spread it on toast, add it to your breakfast muesli and mix it into salad dressings. When you combine tahini with honey you can make halva, which is heavenly.

Hummus

Mashing the chick peas makes them easier to digest. The tahini adds flavour and increases the protein value of the dish.

1 x 400 g tin of pre-cooked chick peas *rinsed & drained*

1 tbsp tahini

2 garlic cloves *crushed*

½ tsp salt

black pepper *to taste*

1 tbsp extra virgin olive oil

1 tbsp linseed oil

1 lemon *juiced*

80 ml water *approximately*

sprinkle of ground paprika & parsley

Place the chick peas, tahini, garlic, salt, oils and lemon juice in a blender.

Blend while adding enough water to make a firm paste.

Season with pepper. Garnish with the paprika and the parsley.

HEMP SEEDS are an excellent source of omega-3 and 6 essential fatty acids, provided in the perfect ratio for maximum absorption by humans. They are also one of nature's best forms of plant-based protein. Hemp protein is more easily digestible than meat, eggs, cheese or cows' milk. What's more, it's a complete protein as it contains all the essential amino acids, so there is no requirement to combine it with grains or pulses as you need to do with other seeds. Hemp is extremely nutritious—a superfood in the truest sense. Allergic reactions to hemp seem to be rare, so it can be useful for people who cannot tolerate nuts, grains or seeds.

Apart from its nutritional benefits it has been used for centuries to make canvas and rope. It can also be an efficient source of fibre for paper, composite plastics, building materials and biofuel.

Hemp has an important historical significance, especially for Americans. Hemp ropes and canvas powered the great sailing ships that traversed the oceans to discover the New World and later transport the first settlers. The US Declaration of Independence was printed on hemp paper.

Another pillar of American civilisation, Levi Strauss, originally made his jeans out of hemp canvas. It was a common US crop even before production was increased during World War II. Since then its rapid demise has been due to its intoxicating cousin: cannabis. This narcotic relative has tarnished the reputation of the respectable hemp. Hemp itself is innocent enough. It is very low in the psychoactive chemical tetrahydrocannabinol (THC), and therefore doesn't produce a narcotic effect*. Unfortunately it seems that just being related to outlaws can damage your reputation. Its association with cannabis has meant that the growing and sale of hemp is not permitted in some countries.

However over the last few decades there has been renewed interest in this versatile plant. It's much easier to grow than cotton, requiring less water and fertiliser. It also needs very little in the way of pesticides because it is naturally anti-fungal and anti-bacterial.

*Keith's warning** The trace amounts of THC in hemp can lead you to fail a drug test, so be aware of this if you are thinking about eating hemp seeds or oil.

ALMONDS have been grown for thousands of years in the Middle East and southern Europe. The original wild bitter almonds were poisonous. But at some point the modern-day sweet and edible almond was cultivated, thankfully.

Almonds are often referred to in the Bible. In fact, Moses' father, Aaron, had a wooden staff that was an almond rod. It sprouted with sweet almonds on one side and bitter almonds on the other. This symbolised the choice his followers could make—the righteous path represented by the sweet almonds or the path of ignorance represented by the toxic bitter almonds.

European settlers took almonds to the USA, where California became the main place of cultivation. Each almond flower needs to be individually pollinated, creating one of the world's biggest migrations of 80 billion animals! Every year over a million beehives are shipped into the Californian almond groves to facilitate the pollination. There isn't much honey though—almond flowers have a lot of pollen, but not much nectar.

The bees need to eat all the honey they produce themselves. Afterwards the bees are shipped back to areas where there are lots of wild flowers for a well earned rest.

CASHEWS The cashew tree originated in Brazil and was taken to India by the Portuguese. From there, its cultivation spread through Asia and Africa. Cashew trees are very sensitive to frost so only grow in the tropics.

Cashew nuts are the seeds from the cashew apple. Popular with the locals, the apples can be eaten raw, or used to make juices and jams.

The shell of the cashew nut is toxic so has to be removed—a laborious process that has to be done by hand, which is why cashews are quite expensive.

Cashews are higher in starch than most other nuts so are used to thicken sauces. They are popular in curries in Goa. The nuts can be salted and roasted to make a delicious snack, or ground into cashew nut butter.

Paneer Delight

The combination of paneer, milk and cashew sauce creates a deliciously rich dish. The cashews are high in starch so act as a natural thickener for the sauce. You could add more vegetables to give extra colour.

Serves 3

250 g paneer *diced*

4 tbsp ghee

1 onion *finely chopped*

2 garlic cloves *crushed*

1 tbsp grated fresh ginger

1 small green chilli
deseeded & finely chopped

1 tsp ground cumin

2 tsp ground coriander

1 tsp garam masala

1 tsp ground paprika

200 ml passata

100 g cashew pieces

150 ml milk

200 ml water

1 tsp grated jaggery *optional*

½ tsp salt

3 tbsp chopped fresh coriander

In a frying pan melt 3 tablespoons of the ghee, add the onion and fry gently for 5–10 minutes until they start to become transparent. Add the ginger, garlic and chilli and cook for 2–3 minutes.

Stir in the passata, mix well and cook until the ghee separates from the tomato mixture. Add the ground cumin, ground coriander and garam masala.

Meanwhile blend the cashews and the milk together in a food processor. Add this to the tomato mix and stir well.

Stir in the water, salt and jaggery. Bring to the boil.

In a frying pan, gently sauté the cubed paneer in the remaining 1 tablespoon of ghee until light gold/brown in colour. Drain the excess ghee and add to the cashew mix.

Garnish with the chopped coriander and a few additional cashews.

LINSEEDS The cultivation of linseed, or flax seed, extends back to before ancient Egyptian times. Its botanical name is *linum usitatissimum*, meaning 'most useful plant'. It was mainly used for fibre and linen before cotton became popular. The kitchen floor covering lino (linoleum) was made from thickened linseed oil.

Linseed oil is very nutritious, being high in omega-3 essential fatty acids. It's not just good as a food—it's also excellent for treating wood. So the humble linseed has provided food, cloth, flooring and fibre.

The flax flower is the emblem of Northern Ireland, where its fibre is used to make Irish linen. Linen is cool and fresh in hot weather. Egyptian mummies were wrapped in linen to represent purity and wealth.

Linseeds can also be used medicinally to make flax tea (see opposite page).

My delicious Super Seed Pickle is high in omega-3 essential fatty acids. It could also be thought of as a spicy Ayurvedic nut butter. It's best made in small batches and stored refrigerated in a jar. You'll need a good grinder or liquidiser.

Keith's Super Seed Pickle

50 g linseeds

50 g sesame seeds *roasted*

50 g almonds *roasted*

25 g tamarind

7 garlic cloves

2 tbsp linseed oil or hemp oil

½ tsp chilli powder

½ tsp Himalayan salt

Roast the garlic for 25 minutes at 175°C. Allow to cool, then remove the skins.

Use a food processor to grind the raw linseeds, sesame seeds and almonds into a fine powder.

Add the tamarind, linseed/hemp oil, peeled garlic, chilli powder and salt. Blend until smooth.

Store in the fridge.

LINSEED TEA HYDRATION

Drinking linseed tea, having a healthy diet and managing your stress is a sound basis for good health.

Linseed tea is highly therapeutic as it's so hydrating. The need for better levels of hydration has been well documented. Minor dehydration is the hidden cause of many illnesses. Water around the cells is like oil in an engine; without it they can't function properly. Even if you have a great diet, your body can't take advantage of it if you are dehydrated.

The answer is to drink more, but if you are stressed your body can behave like a badly watered hanging basket. The water just goes straight through, hardly touching the sides!

Linseed tea helps because it is slightly gelatinous so it soothes and relaxes the colon, enabling it to absorb more water. The tea's viscosity means the water will remain longer in the colon, and be absorbed better. It's exactly the same principle as the special hanging basket compost which contains gel to hold the water in the soil for longer.

Another benefit of linseed tea is that it will hydrate your skin, so you'll look better. Horse owners have always fed their animals linseeds to give them a shiny coat, and it can work for us too!

The tea is made by boiling a few linseeds in water and drinking the resulting stock. Ideally it needs to be just a bit thicker than water and have a faint nutty taste. If you use too many seeds it comes out very 'gloopy'; but don't worry, you can dilute it with more hot water.

Linseed Tea

This is a really simple recipe. Mix 1 teaspoon of linseeds with 1 litre of water. Bring to the boil and then let it stand for 20 minutes. Discard the seeds and drink the water. You can add hot water to dilute it to taste, especially if it's too gelatinous.

FAVOURITE VEGETABLES

COURGETTE This popular vegetable is related to squash plants brought to Europe from South America. Bred over some generations, this is a fairly recently developed vegetable from about 125 years ago. It originated in Italy where it is called zucchini which literally means 'little squash'. Courgette is the French name which is widely used in the UK, and by us in this book.

We use a lot of courgettes because they are easy to cut and cook quickly. They are very versatile and can be fried, sautéed, steamed or baked. If we ever start running out of food it's easy to make a quick tomato sauce, fry some courgettes in olive oil and add a bit of tofu for a 5 minute dish. Handy when there is a queue of hungry people!

In the UK, big courgettes are called marrows. They change as they grow—the skin gets tougher, the flesh becomes softer and there are many large seeds in the middle. They can be sliced into rings, deseeded and baked with delicious fillings, or just steamed and served with butter and black pepper.

CAULIFLOWER The cauliflower came into being in the Middle East, cultivated from wild varieties of cabbage. It first appeared in Europe about 800 years ago and became popular in France during the 1600s. The normal white colour of the florets provides a great contrast to the greens, reds and oranges of other vegetables. Cauliflower was introduced to India in the 1800s by Europeans and is now one of their most important winter crops. We use it a lot as a steamed vegetable served with a creamy cheesy sauce. Then I'm in heaven! The cauliflower is also a favourite in my spicy Indian dishes.

BROCCOLI, or calabrese, is named after its place of origin. Calabria is in Italy, and broccolo means 'the flowering head of a cabbage'. It was first cultivated by the Romans and has remained popular in Italy ever since. It was brought to the UK in the 18th century and used occasionally as an exotic vegetable. Its long journey to fame started when it was taken to the USA by Italian immigrants, and by the 1920s it was more widely known. Broccoli's popularity spread to the rest of Europe soon after.

Green and tree-like, it looks fantastic on the plate. Easy to cook and delicious, it's a cabbage family favourite. Even children will 'eat their greens' if you give them freshly steamed broccoli.

My wife's favourite method is to melt some butter in a pan, then add a handful of sliced leeks along with the broccoli. This she sautés for about a minute. She then adds some stock, covers the pan and cooks it gently until the broccoli's just right: soft but not soggy, crunchy but not raw.

SWEET POTATO Like butternut squash, sweet potato is a very versatile ingredient. It is delicious and easy to cook and tastes good even without the addition of other ingredients. The cook just has to be careful not to add any flavours that mess it up!

The name 'potato' comes from the native word for sweet potato, 'batatas', which became 'patatas' in Spanish. In their native South America there are many varieties of cultivated sweet potato which vary in colour, from reddish orange to white, but only a few are edible. Those with colour are sweeter than the ones with white flesh.

Sweet potatoes were exported from South America to Asia well before European contact. Polynesian traders brought them across the Pacific to New Zealand and from there they reached Japan and Korea.

Like the spud, sweet potatoes are cheap, easy to grow and nutritious, and have become popular as a staple food in warm climates all over the world.

SWEDE This is a shortened version of its original name 'Swedish cabbage'. It was created in Sweden from a cross between turnip and cabbage. In Scotland they are called neeps, and a favourite national dish is 'neeps and tatties' which is swede and potato. They are boiled seperately, mashed with butter and served side by side.

Many of our European visitors aren't familiar with this hardy vegetable, as in a lot of countries they are just used to feed cattle. But this tough little root is surprisingly good, and becomes sweeter and more orange as you cook it.

I love it mashed with butter and fresh ground pepper. It is also great in soups and stews with other root vegetables. It is not so good roasted as it tend to get a bit dry and tough.

SPINACH was first known in Persia and spread from there to India and China, and around 800 AD it started to make an appearance in Europe. It became popular because it grows early in spring before a lot of other crops are ready. For this reason it became an important food in 'the hungry gap' when the winter foods were running out but summer ones not yet ripe.

Florentine is a word used to describe dishes with spinach, like egg florentine. This started because spinach was popularised in France by the Italian wife of the French King Henry II, Catherine de Medici, who came from Florence.

Popeye the Sailor Man relied on spinach to give him extra strength. This was based on a faulty calculation by Emil von Wolff who, when calculating the iron content of spinach in 1870, put the decimal point in the wrong place so he recorded 10 times the actual level of iron. This error was not noticed until 1930. By then the popular misconception was well and truly established.

AUBERGINE The name aubergine has a French origin. Its common name is eggplant, so called because the original varieties were smaller and white coloured—just like eggs. Aubergines are from the same family as potatoes and tomatoes, but originally came from India where they have been cultivated for thousands of years. From there they spread to the Middle East and Europe. They didn't reach Britain properly until the 17th century. Indian aubergines are much smaller than their Western cousins.

CARROT Carrots were originally grown for their seeds and leaves, like the closely related plants dill, cumin and fennel. As a root vegetable, it didn't taste great. It was later cultivated to make its roots sweeter and less woody.

The original carrot that came from Persia and Afghanistan about a thousand years ago was a purple colour. Even today, carrots in India are a pinky red.

They became popular in Europe in the 1600s, and the familiar orange carrot was cultivated in the Netherlands as a patriotic gesture to the Dutch Royal Family whose symbolic colour is orange. This dates back to William of Orange who founded the modern state of The Netherlands. Carrots are probably the most successful example of vegetable propaganda! These nationalistic roots spread all over Europe and were then taken, by European settlers, across the Atlantic to the USA.

During World War II the carrot was again employed as a political agent, this time by the British. The bright colour of carrots is due to their beta carotene content. This can be converted by the body into vitamin A which is needed for good eyesight. It was publicised that pilots were eating more carrots so they could see better in the dark, while really they were using radar. My family took this information to heart, and as a child I had to eat lots of carrots 'to help with my night vision'.

The more politically neutral and original 'wild carrot' is still an important herbal remedy. It is used as a kidney tonic in the same way as parsley.

ONION We don't use onions and garlic very much at the Dru Centre because in yoga philosophy they are considered 'rajasic'. This means they encourage excess stimulation of the mind and senses, and can counteract the calming effect of yoga and meditation. In Ayurveda, too, they are pungent in taste, thought to increase activity in our mind and emotions.

However, cooking the onions sweetens the taste and lessens the stimulating effect. So if I do use them, I cook them quite well. Also if you are feeling sluggish, pungent foods like onions can be helpful to stimulate your mind and body.

Onions and garlic are both therapeutic, and are used by herbalists to help with mild infections. In Ayurveda they say anything edible can be a food, a medicine or a poison. In this case onions can be used as all three—a medicine in home remedies, a delicious food in recipes or a poison if your mind or body is already overactive or agitated.

Certainly on our advanced meditation courses we tend not to use them at all, but otherwise we use them in moderation as they are delicious in so many dishes. I sometimes grind them with ginger in a food processor to make a great curry paste and thickener.

The cultivation of onions goes back to ancient Egypt. They revered them and saw the concentric rings as a spiritual symbol of creation. Onion rings were placed over the eyes of the deceased at burials—much cheaper than the ancient Roman tradition of using coins.

Onions are a great home remedy. Like garlic they may help prevent heart disease and act as a natural antibiotic.

'An onion a day keeps arteriosclerosis at bay,' says Dr Victor Gurewich, Director of the Tufts University Vascular Laboratory in Boston. He knows his onions, having researched their therapeutic effects.

Curry Paste

You can use this curry paste in vegetable or pulse dishes.
You can also use it as a marinade or for freshening up
leftovers from a previous meal.

WHOLE SPICES

2 tbsp ghee

10 cm cinnamon stick

12 black peppercorns

2 tsp cumin seeds

5 cardamoms

3 cloves

1 bay leaf

GROUND SPICES

1 tbsp ground coriander

1 tsp ground turmeric

1 tsp garam masala

1 tsp ground paprika

2 tbsp tomato purée

100 ml water

salt *to taste*

FOR GRINDING

1 onion *chopped*

4 cm fresh ginger *peeled*

8 garlic cloves *peeled*

Blend the onion, ginger and garlic in a food processor until smooth.

Heat the ghee in a large frying pan. Add the whole spices and fry until they start to crackle. Add the onion paste and mix in the salt.

Cover the pan and simmer gently and slowly for at least 5 minutes.

Add all of the ground spices and mix well. Add the water and the tomato purée. Cook for another 5 minutes or until the ghee separates slightly from the sauce.

CELERY Like carrots, celery was a popular vegetable in classical Greek and Egyptian times. The seeds were used for cooking and as a medicine. Originally the leaves and stem were less popular and would have been much smaller and more bitter than the celery we are familiar with today. It wasn't until the 1600s that, through seed selection, the vegetable was bred to be larger and sweeter.

Celeriac is a variety of celery with a large bulb. A root vegetable, it is great in soups and stews. Celery seeds are a spice and can be ground with salt to make celery salt. This is also used medicinally as a diuretic and digestive herb.

Celery is surprisingly popular with some football fans—not to eat, but to throw at the opposing team when taking corners. It may seem like a strange activity, but the weighty base and feathery leaves make celery surprisingly aerodynamic. It could even become a sport in its own right! At one important football match, the game had to be stopped while celery was cleared from the pitch. You aren't allowed to take celery into a match any more, even if you're on a diet. Celery has a connection with a certain football club, where fans even target their own goalie on 'salad days'.

CABBAGE The cabbages we know today were cultivated from leafy plants growing near the seashore as they are salt-tolerant and resistant to dry and salty conditions. Cabbage is a biennial crop. It is normally harvested as a vegetable in the first year, and flowers and goes to seed in the second.

The first cabbages were simple leafy types and were used as a food as far back as Classical times. The now familiar headed varieties were developed later and first recorded in the late Middle Ages when they became a popular and staple food in Europe.

Cabbages, like cauliflowers, were taken by spice traders to Asia where they were cultivated as a winter crop.

TOMATO Tomatoes came from Mexico and this is more or less their authentic Aztec name, 'tomati'. They were originally small and yellow and were hence called 'golden apples' by the Europeans.

Tomatoes were viewed at first with some suspicion due to their similarity to the common garden weed, deadly nightshade, which is poisonous, so they didn't really take off in Europe until the 17th and 18th centuries.

The Spanish took the tomato to the Philippines where it was cultivated and spread to other Asian countries. Since the 1950s the modern tomato has been bred for shape and colour at the expense of taste.

I love the tomatoes in Bulgaria as they have their own varieties which have not been bred for looks alone. They are often misshapen by our standards but taste delicious.

ROCKET is derived from the French name Rouchette. Although it's been popular in Italy since Roman times it has only recently become commonplace in Britain. There is nothing nicer than a really fresh bowl of rocket salad. In Italy, rocket leaves are often sprinkled on fresh pasta or pizza just before serving.

It's great mixed with dandelion leaves. Dandelion comes from the French 'dent de lion', literally the 'lion's tooth' which the leaf resembles. The bitter taste of rocket and dandelion is stimulating for your liver and digestion.

CAPSICUM These are also called bell peppers because the hotter varieties taste similar to peppercorns, though the two are not related. The capsicum's peppery taste evolved to appeal to birds who distributed the seeds. Unlike most mammals, birds are not sensitive to the taste. Also unlike many mammals, birds have good colour vision and so were attracted to the specially evolved bright colours. We humans are one of the few mammals that have taken a liking to the pungent taste and bright tones of capsicums as, like birds, we have good colour vision.

But perhaps the plant has had the last laugh as we have taken it from its native South America and distributed and cultivated it all over the world.

I use capsicums to add colour to all sorts of dishes, and they are a key ingredient in my Mojo sauce recipe. A gift to any cook, they add colour and a delicate flavour and, like courgettes, are easy and quick to prepare.

CHILLI PEPPERS These are the hot variety of pepper, probably named after their country of origin, Chile. They became popular quite quickly when they reached Europe. Chilli peppers offered a cheap alternative to peppercorns, which were very expensive at the time (so much so that they were even used as a form of currency).

The Portuguese took chillies from South America to their colonies in Asia, particularly Goa in India—home of the vindaloo curry.

Chilli is an important herbal remedy. It will open up tissues and increase the flow of blood. Chilli tincture as a stimulant is a good substitute for coffee—a few drops on the tongue will bring blood to the head and stimulate the adrenal glands.

At the Dru Centre we use chillies very sparingly. Like onions and garlic they are overstimulating for some people. Also they tend to irritate rather than stimulate the digestive tract. We use black pepper to strengthen the digestion instead.

BUTTERNUT SQUASH

This vegetable was developed in the 1940s by Charles Leggett from the USA. He cross-bred two varieties of squash with a great result. He called it 'butternut' squash because of its buttery and nutty taste. This wonderful vegetable was the result of his experiments even though Mr Leggett wasn't an experienced plant breeder or farmer. He said it was a gift from the gods. We agree and use it almost every day as it's easy to cook and is always delicious. It can be roasted or boiled, and can be cooked with pulses to make a great soup or bake.

Removing the skin can be quite hard work, so you need a good peeler. You can also leave the skin on; it goes quite soft and chewy when cooked. Or you can easily peel it after it's cooked and has cooled down.

GARLIC is incredibly therapeutic. During the Great Plague in Europe, four thieves made a dubious living by robbing the houses of victims. Yet how did they survive the plague themselves?

Once caught, they revealed their secret formula, which contained garlic and protected them from the disease. Unfortunately it was no protection from the punishment that followed. If only they had patented the remedy and sold it instead.

Four Thieves Vinegar

There are many variations of this recipe which has traditionally been used as a medicine, a disinfectant spray and an insect repellent. It also inspired the recipe for the popular 'Thieves' essential oil blend—an aromatherapy oil used externally for similar purposes. For the following traditional recipe you can use dried herbs and flowers or fresh if they are available. Garlic is the most active ingredient and is supported by the other herbs.

TRADITIONAL USES

For immune boosting: 1–2 tablespoons were mixed with 1 tablespoon of raw honey and taken once a day. As a disinfectant: the vinegar was sprayed onto surfaces and wiped clean with a cloth. As an insect repellent: it was diluted with 3 parts water to 1 part vinegar and applied using a spray bottle.

2 garlic cloves *peeled & finely sliced*

3 fresh lavender flowers

3 tips fresh rosemary

3 tips fresh mint

3 tips fresh sage

3 tips fresh marjoram

3 tips fresh thyme

3 tips fresh parsley

500 ml cider vinegar

Mix all the ingredients together in a glass jar.

Cover with a watertight lid.

Leave it to marinate for 7 days in a sunny location. If there's no sun, leave for 10 days.

Every day put your love and healing intention into it by gently shaking the jar.

When it's ready, strain the Four Thieves Vinegar through a fine sieve into another jar or bottle.

Store in the fridge and use within a month.

Wild garlic is common in woodlands, often growing near water. Like bluebells, garlic flowers before the trees are fully in leaf and fills the air with a fragrant, if slightly garlicky, aroma. The leaves are edible and can be used as a salad. It is also called 'bear garlic' because brown bears love to eat it in the spring. If you have ever smelt their breath, you will know this is one case where garlic actually improves it and makes it bearable.

Garlic can really help with any cold. It stops the virus from spreading because everyone keeps away from you. Unfortunately it's the aromatic bits that work, so deodorised garlic capsules can be less effective. Garlic is a powerful antibiotic, commonly used before modern drugs were developed. It was known as Russian penicillin as it was commonly used there as a remedy.

Keith's warning If you are going to pick your own garlic leaves, be careful because they look similar to other plant leaves that can be quite poisonous.

Russian Penicillin

4 garlic cloves *peeled & chopped*

1 grapefruit *sliced with peel*

1 lemon *sliced with peel*

1 medium onion *finely chopped*

1 ltr water

½ tsp chilli powder

Makes 1 day's supply

Place all the ingredients, apart from the chilli, in a pan and pour in the water. Bring to the boil, cover and simmer for about 10 minutes.

Add the chilli powder during the last couple of minutes of cooking.

Leave to cool.

Pour through a tea strainer to serve. Drink a small glass 3 times a day for colds or flu.

There is an Islamic legend that when Satan left the Garden of Eden, from one footprint grew the garlic and from the other, the onion.

There is a similar more gruesome Hindu story. The gods were looking for the essence of immortality. They were instructed to churn a great ocean of milk. After some time the elixir of life came out as nectar. Secretly a hidden demon managed to drink some. When the gods realised this they quickly cut off his head to stop him becoming immortal. The spilt blood grew into the garlic plant, which has both medicinal and demonic qualities.

It was too late to stop the demon as he had already drunk the nectar. He now lived on as two parts—a living head and a separate tail! He eternally takes his revenge on the uncharitable deities by swallowing either the sun god or the moon god to create an eclipse.

Like onions, garlic is a delicious food and herb, as well as being an effective medicine. Again, like the onion, it can be overstimulating for certain personality types and so we use it sparingly during many of our courses.

Keith's tip These traditional herbal formulas are provided for your information only. Please get advice from a qualified practitioner before using herbs therapeutically.

LETTUCE The ancient Egyptians turned a medicinal weed into a vegetable cultivated for its leaves. Wild lettuce is a mild sedative and can be used to promote sleep.

It spread to Rome where it was called lactuca, the word for 'milk', as a milky latex exudes from the stem when it is cut. Lettuce became more popular in Europe after the 1700s, and a worldwide crop over the last hundred years.

I use a lot of cos lettuce (also called Romany lettuce). It may have derived its name from the Island of Kos as a lot of lettuce used to be cultivated there. I like it because it is crisp and can tolerate a warm dressing.

BEETROOT is derived from sea beet which grows wild on the Mediterranean coast. It is an ancient Egyptian vegetable that can be traced as far back as 2,000 BC. Both the leaves and root were common foods in Roman times and in Medieval Europe.

Beetroot has long been used as a herbal remedy and nutritious food. It is high in iron and other vitamins and minerals.

The Romans used beetroot juice as an aphrodisiac. Now, in alternative medicine, beetroot is used regularly in juice therapy and as a blood purifier. The red colour in beetroot not only stains clothes, but also passes right through your system and can be mistaken for blood in the urine.

CUCUMBER The cucumber has been cultivated in India for 3,000 years and from there it reached ancient Greece and Rome. It was so popular with the Romans that they set up greenhouses to make cucumber available all year round.

The vegetable spread through the rest of Europe much later. Raw food was discouraged in the late 17th century so cucumbers were mainly fed to animals and were called cowcombers, which is where the modern name came from.

Cucumber is a traditional herbal remedy used to soothe the urinary tract. It is also used as an anti-wrinkle cream when liquidised with yoghurt.

LEEKS Our main Dru Centre is in the Welsh county of Gwynedd. It was here around 600 AD that the local king ordered his soldiers to identify themselves by wearing leeks on their helmets. To this day the Welsh Guards Regiment still wear a leek on their headgear, but now it is a badge with a leek design rather than the actual vegetable. Leeks are still one of the symbols of Wales, equivalent to the thistle of Scotland, the rose of England and the shamrock of Ireland.

In our kitchen we use leeks as a milder, less heating and stimulating alternative to onions or garlic. Leeks are delicious as part of a stock or stew, and also superb as a fresh vegetable. I love them freshly steamed and served with butter.

Leeks are a fantastic winter vegetable crop, available until they flower and seed in early springtime. Leeks are popular in Scotland too, and are in one of their national dishes 'Cock-a-Leekie Soup'. For this dish, most people keep the chicken and leave out the prunes. In my vegetarian version I keep the prunes and leave out the chicken.

Cock-a-Leekie Soup

1 tbsp ghee or coconut oil

200 g carrots *chopped*

2 celery sticks *chopped*

1 leek *washed & cut into thick rounds (with the green tops)*

2 bay leaves

100 g swede *diced*

750 ml vegetable stock

1 tbsp chopped fresh thyme

6 prunes *stones removed*

salt & pepper *to taste*

Serves 4

Heat the ghee/coconut oil in a large heavy-based saucepan. Sauté the carrots, celery and leek for 5 minutes until they start to brown.

Cover with stock and add the swede, bay leaves, thyme and prunes. Slowly bring to the boil. Simmer for 20 minutes or until the vegetables are tender. Season to taste.

APPLE The apple is a member of the rose family, originating in Central Asia. In fact, the name of the biggest city in Kazakhstan, Almaty, literally means 'apple'. This was well before New York became known as 'the Big Apple' in the United States.

Apples have been an important food for thousands of years. They store well over winter if kept in a cool and frost-free place.

They also have a lot of spiritual and religious significance. The temptation of the apple in the Garden of Eden banished us all to our present earthly and mortal life. Apples are the symbol of Venus and love.

In ancient Greece a suitor would throw an apple to his beloved. If she caught it, it meant the feeling was mutual.

One of the 12 labours of Hercules was to pick the golden apples from the tree of life in the garden of Hesperides. He needed the help of Atlas, who was related to Hesperides, so Hercules held the Earth while Atlas went to fetch the apples.

On returning, Atlas decided he enjoyed his freedom so suggested that he finish the task while Hercules continue holding the Earth. Hercules agreed but asked Atlas to hold the Earth temporarily so he could adjust his robe. Hercules then ran off with the apples, leaving Atlas stranded in his eternal role.

Hippomenes used golden apples to outrun the beautiful Atlanta in a race. She had declared that any man who won could marry her, but a loser would forfeit his life. A few suitors had already tried and failed, so Hippomenes was not prepared to take any chances. Each time she raced ahead of him he threw a golden apple, which he knew she would find irresistible and would leave the race to go and collect it. He had to do this three times to finally win the race and claim his bride.

CUPBOARD INGREDIENTS

VEGETABLE STOCK A good stock really adds flavour to all sorts of dishes. You can make your own by simmering vegetables such as garlic, carrots, onions and celery, then straining off the juice.

I often use Marigold bouillon powder. It contains a delicious herb called lovage, which looks like a large celery plant and grows well in gardens. Originally known as 'love herb', lovage was thought to be an aphrodisiac, hence the name. You only need a little to make a soup or stew taste extra special.

I try to reduce waste by making a stock from the peelings of washed vegetables—like the tops of leeks and the bases of celery. By doing this I can use the parts of the vegetables that are usually thrown away.

Keith's Vegetable Stock

'WASTE' INGREDIENTS

outer layers & root of onions *washed*

top & tail of carrots

base & outer leaves of celery

green tops of leeks

potato peelings

sweet potato peelings

PLUS

2 ltrs water

1 tsp chopped fresh thyme

1 bay leaf

1 tbsp chopped fresh parsley

10 peppercorns

Place the ingredients in a large pan and cover with the water.

Bring to the boil and simmer for an hour or so, keeping the vegetables covered with water. Strain off the stock and use in soups or stews.

SALT How ironic that salt, which is essential to life, is now viewed with suspicion. In fact, salt is a very important nutrient. In Bulgaria and Russia its life-giving properties are well respected. Honoured guests are presented with ceremonial bread and salt. Even in space! When astronauts arrived at the International Space Station, the Russians greeted them in the traditional way with bread and salt.

Nowadays salt has become something we are told to more or less avoid. Excessive use of refined, sodium-rich salt in processed foods is harmful. The process of refining salt strips it of nearly all minerals except the sodium chloride itself.

However unrefined salt is an essential mineral and an important Ayurvedic taste. A little salt added to natural food enhances its flavour and digestibility. With vegetarian food you may need to add some salt, as vegetables tend to have a lower salt content than meat or fish.

You can also make it go further by using my Six Taste Spice Mix (page 270) which

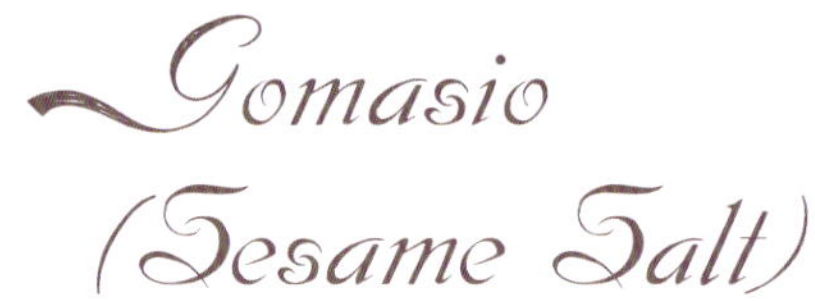

Gomasio (Sesame Salt)

2 tbsp sesame seeds
½ tsp salt

Dry roast the sesame seeds in a frying pan over a medium heat, stirring until light golden in colour.

Add the salt, stir and cook for about 30 seconds. Then allow to cool.

Grind with a pestle and mortar or grinder. Use instead of salt at the table.

includes salt, or by using sesame salt (gomasio) which is roasted sesame seeds ground with salt. In Japan they use soy sauce or tamari (fermented soya) for its salty taste.

My favourite salt is Himalayan salt, which has a pink colour due to its rich and varied mineral content.

THE PROBLEM WITH SUGAR

Sugar unfortunately, like salt, is now so widely misused it has become a major cause of ill health.

In Ayurveda, sugar is generally viewed as an immune system suppressant, although a small amount of jaggery (pure, dried sugar cane juice) can be used to enhance the sweet taste in food.

Sugar used to be an expensive luxury, but in the 1400s improved refining techniques meant sugar became cheaper and more widely available. Lots of sugar plantations were established in tropical regions, including the Canary Islands. It was from there that Christopher Columbus took some plants on his first voyage to America in 1492. By the 1700s increasingly efficient processing techniques meant that sugar became a normal part of people's diets.

The detrimental effects of sugar are well documented. The problem with refined sugar is that it's had all its trace minerals and nutrients removed, making it extremely difficult for the body to utilise properly—this is what makes sugar harmful. In fact, most people who try to eat healthily avoid refined sugar completely.

Sugar will leach the minerals from your body as it is metabolised. If the rest of your diet is lacking in minerals, eating sugar will exacerbate the situation.

In addition, sugar raises your blood sugar quickly to an unnaturally high level. It then plummets rapidly to an even lower level than before. This creates further sugar cravings, so you just end up eating more and more of this calorie-rich but nutrient-poor food. Even so-called 'raw sugar' has had a lot of its nutrients removed to produce molasses—which is then sold separately as a health food.

Jaggery is a nutrient-rich wholesome food

JAGGERY SUGAR CANE JUICE

I like to use natural sweeteners like jaggery which is dried sugar cane juice. It comes from India and is often made in the fields where the sugar crop is grown. The sugar cane is crushed and the juice evaporated in big cauldrons. The fire is fuelled by the discarded sugar cane stems and the juice boiled until it sets. It is then sold in blocks.

Jaggery is much healthier than refined sugar because it is richer in nutrients and is therefore more naturally satisfying.

Sugar cane was originally called 'honey stick', and people used to just chew the fibres for the sweet taste. Another name for it is 'khanda', which is where the word 'candy' comes from.

The commercial production of jaggery was first recorded in about 500 AD. Unlike fresh sugar cane, jaggery can be stored and easily transported. Interestingly, crystallised sugar production also started in India. Both jaggery and refined sugar became valuable commodities, globally traded like spices.

Mahatma Gandhi noted that the Indian people had used jaggery for generations as a healthy and wholesome food. However, by the 1900s it had been largely replaced by refined white sugar which was often imported. He campaigned for a return to the natural form of jaggery which was nutritious and could be produced locally.

If you can't find jaggery in your local shops, you should be able to order it online.

COCONUT SUGAR

A possible substitute for jaggery is coconut sugar, which is made from the sap of the coconut palm, and is prepared in the same way as jaggery. Coconut sugar is available in most health shops and comes in a granular form which is easy to use.

HONEY was the first and original natural sweetener and superfood. Honey bees have been semi-domesticated for thousands of years; even the earliest cave paintings show people harvesting wild honey.

Bees really are busy. They fly the equivalent of a round-the-world trip to make just one jar of honey. This includes visiting around two million flowers, which takes about 20,000 bee trips. But it's not all work and no play—there's still time to dance. Bee dances are not only a welcome break, but also tell other bees where they can find good flowers.

Even at home in the hive there's work to be done. The (most probably) exhausted bees have to fan the collected nectar with their wings to make the liquid evaporate and the nectar condense into honey. The honey then has to be carefully stored away in the wax honeycomb.

To collect the honey, beekeepers smoke the hive. This tricks the bees into thinking there is a forest fire so they evacuate the hive. Beekeepers then take any excess honey, leaving enough behind for the bees to eat themselves.

Like jaggery, natural raw honey is a sweet that is healthy. Not only does it have all the nutrients we need to digest it, but it is a medicine too. Honey has natural antibacterial and antifungal qualities.

Unlike refined sugar, which is acidic, raw honey is alkaline so helps reduce acidity in the body.

Honey also lessens the pain from cuts and stings—which is useful if not all the bees fall for the smoking trick when you're trying to collect the honey in the first place.

Honey is used as a carrier for Ayurvedic medicinal herbs. Not only does a spoonful of honey help the medicine go down, it can also make it stronger and more effective.

French Honey & Cheese

Heat the milk in a pan until it boils. Remove from the heat and add the lemon juice. After a few minutes, strain the curds through a fine sieve lined with muslin or cheesecloth.

Allow the curds to cool then mix in the cream cheese until it forms a smooth paste. Chill, then serve on dessert plates. Garnish each mound with the toasted walnuts and 2 tablespoons of honey.

500 ml milk
½ lemon juiced
100 g Chèvre goat cheese (cream cheese)
125 g walnuts toasted
120 ml raw honey

YOGHURT The history of yoghurt goes back to ancient times. The earliest probably formed spontaneously by the action of naturally occurring bacteria. The health benefits this process yielded were soon greatly appreciated. Firstly, yoghurt will keep fresh much longer than milk and is easier to digest. Even people who are lactose intolerant can sometimes eat yoghurt as most of the lactose in it gets transformed into other sugars by the bacteria.

Yoghurt is sour, which is an important taste in Ayurveda as it stimulates digestion. Sourness also increases salivation and hence the absorption of minerals.

But the main thing about yoghurt is that it's full of bacteria! This may not sound very appetising but these are healthy bugs that promote beneficial micro-organisms in the gut. This is incredibly important. The wrong bacteria can reduce absorption of food and actually produce toxins, sometimes causing irritation in the bowel which may lead to allergies. Basically, food can go off inside us before we have a chance to absorb it.

On the other hand, good bacteria improve conditions in the gut. They create a healthy environment that increases absorption and digestibility. Yoghurt is full of these healthy bacteria and helps promote conditions for them to settle and thrive in the digestive system.

It's important to use live yoghurts rather than those that are pasteurised or heat-treated to kill the bacteria—a process that defeats the object a bit. Yoghurt is most potent when it is fresh and the bacteria are vibrant and alive. Chilling and storage make it less active and also harder to digest. Ayurveda does not generally recommend eating cold foods unless the weather is very warm, or you have a hot constitution. Although we need to refrigerate dairy produce to keep it safe, I try to let yoghurt get to room temperature before I eat it.

Yoghurt is great in sweet and savoury dishes, and a good source of extra protein. I often use it as a topping on hot food and desserts. This warms up the yoghurt and, we hope, wakes up the healthy bugs.

Yoghurt also has a naturally cooling effect, so it's useful for balancing spicy dishes. If you eat something with too much chilli you instinctively reach for a glass of water, but a spoonful of yoghurt is a much better way to cool your mouth down in a hurry.

Probably the first and best luxury dessert ever invented is fresh yoghurt and honey, the knowledge of which has persisted while great civilisations have risen and fallen. Everything else may have changed but yoghurt and honey has remained a constant delight. It was called food of the gods in ancient India and Greece. The promised 'land of milk and honey' in the Bible may refer to a popular ancient fermented yoghurt and honey drink.

Until the 1900s yoghurt was only known in Asia and Eastern Europe. It steadily became more popular in America following the immigration of Eastern Europeans. With so many health benefits, it became fashionable with naturopaths such as John Kellogg of cornflakes fame. He used it as a health food and in therapeutic enemas. But it wasn't until the 1960s that it really took off as a health food in the West. Interest in this superfood developed when the longevity of Bulgarians was linked to eating yoghurt.

Ayurvedic Lassi

This yoghurt drink is surprisingly refreshing on a hot day. It's also healthier than the more familiar mango lassi we get in Indian restaurants.

200 ml live yoghurt or kefir
100 ml warm water
¼ tsp Himalayan salt
pinch of ground ginger
1 tsp cumin seeds

Makes one large glass
Roast the cumin seeds until fragrant. Grind with a pestle and mortar or a grinder.

Add a pinch of the ground cumin to the yoghurt (store the rest in a jar for next time).

Add the water and other ingredients. Blend well and serve.

CORNFLOUR was invented in the USA in 1840 and used initially as a laundry starch. It was later discovered to be a good food thickener as, like arrowroot, it went clear on heating. It became a popular cooking essential soon after.

It's the main ingredient in Bird's Custard, which was developed at about the same time. Alfred Bird's wife was allergic to eggs, so he tried using cornflour instead. It made his custard easier and cheaper to make and so increased its popularity. Bird's Custard became one of the world's first 'instant' foods. I have a lot of friends who need a gluten-free diet, so I sometimes use cornflour rather than wheat flour as a sauce thickener—you just have to be careful to avoid lumps.

COCONUT MILK Palm trees can produce 70–100 or more coconuts in a year. Nearly all parts of the coconut are nutritionally useful: the water, the milk, the flesh and the oil. Even the leaves and husks of the palm tree itself are used as building materials and for decoration. That is why in Sanskrit the coconut palm is known as 'kalpa vriksha' which literally means 'wish-fulfilling tree'. Coconuts are very healthy, unless you get hit by a falling one, of course.

Coconut milk is not the liquid found in the nut: that is called coconut water. Coconut milk is made from the flesh of the coconut, which is ground up, mixed with water and strained. As in dairy production the fat (cream) rises to the top and is skimmed off as coconut cream. The first pressing is high in fat and called thick coconut milk, used for desserts and thick sauces. The residue is mixed with more water and pressed again—this is thin coconut milk, which is used in soups and savoury dishes.

In Wales we normally get coconut milk in tins. Sometimes the oil separates out and goes solid in the tin and you have to scrape it out. We use a lot of coconut milk as we cater for many people who are vegan or dairy-free. It is creamy like milk and is great in desserts and savoury dishes.

The fat in the coconut milk is very healthy. Some evidence suggests that it may increase your 'good' high-density lipoprotein cholesterol. It's high in lauric acid, which is also thought to be antifungal and antiviral and protects from a wide variety of harmful organisms.

PANCHAMRIT This is a traditional Ayurvedic preparation made from five (panch) ingredients to form the nectar (amrit) of long life.

This Ayurvedic dessert is thought to be blessed with many magical, healing qualities. It is also considered fit to offer to the gods and is used in many Hindu rituals.

The first ingredient is milk, which is white and represents purity.

The second is yoghurt, which traditionally symbolises prosperity.

The third is honey, which signifies sweetness in speech and unity (the bees work together).

Fourth is jaggery, raw sugar cane, to give sweetness in taste and in our lives.

Finally butter ghee, being the finest essence of the milk, represents knowledge.

Panchamrit

There are various recipes for this. Some just use equal quantities of each. I like to do it the traditional way where the ingredients are in decreasing proportions.

100 ml milk

80 ml yoghurt

60 g raw honey

40 g jaggery

20 ml ghee

Serves 4

Bring the milk to the boil.
Add the jaggery and stir until it dissolves.
Allow it to cool until warm. Whisk in the ghee and then the yoghurt and honey.

PANEER has been used in India for thousands of years. It is a simple unfermented cheese that keeps its shape during cooking. Paneer is made by boiling milk, which is then curdled using lemon juice. The mixture is then strained and pressed to form blocks.

Extremely useful as a vegetarian food, paneer is a good source of meat-free protein—delicious and satisfying. It's the only cheese recommended in classical Ayurvedic cooking, as it's light and easy to digest.

Paneer is an unsalted white cheese, with a mild, milky taste. It goes well with the spicy flavours used in Asian dishes. Because it doesn't melt, it can be stirred into soups or curries and remains intact. It is a main ingredient in many classical Indian dishes like saag (spinach) paneer and mattar (peas) paneer. It is an easy way to transform a simple dish into a meal.

It is also great in vegetarian kebabs and barbecues. Paneer is one of the original fast foods (now recognised as such by McDonalds in India, who've added McSpicy Paneer to their menu).

Paneer

1 ltr whole milk

3-4 tbsp lemon juice

Pour the milk into a pan and boil. Reduce the heat and slowly add the lemon juice. Stir the milk as it starts to curdle.

Remove it from the heat and leave it to stand for 10 minutes as the curds completely separate from the whey.

Line a sieve with a piece of muslin and place it over a bowl. Carefully pour the mixture into the sieve and collect the curds in the muslin.

Rinse the curds under a cold tap to get rid of any leftover whey.

Gather the muslin, and squeeze out the excess liquid. Press the bundle by putting some weight on it, about 1 kilo, and leave for at least 15 minutes.

Place the paneer in the fridge for an hour or so to set properly.

MACROBIOTIC INGREDIENTS

TOFU is made like paneer but from curdled soya milk, which is strained and pressed in the same way. Unlike cheese, it tastes a bit bland. But it does soak up other flavours easily. Baked or fried with tamari and seaweed it quickly becomes very tasty.

Like paneer, tofu is an easy way to transform a simple dish into a meal. It is substantial because it has a high protein and fat content. Macrobiotics advises eating tofu with seaweed. This counters tofu's thyroid-lowering effect and neutralises other anti-nutrients found in soya.

TAMARI is a bacteria-fermented soya product. It has a rich, savoury flavour and contains natural B12 and beneficial enzymes that aid digestion.

Genuine tamari is gluten-free as it is the liquid collected at the bottom of the keg during miso production. It has a stronger flavour than 'shoyu' sauce which contains wheat. Cheap, imitation soy sauce can be made from hydrolysed vegetable protein coloured with caramel, and is nutritionally inferior.

TEMPEH Most soya products come from Japan or China, but tempeh originated in Java so it's popular in spicy Indonesian dishes. Tempeh is made from fermented soya beans which are pressed into blocks.

It can be used like tofu but has a strong flavour of its own. The big benefit is that it is pre-digested by healthy bacteria.

Keith's tip Soya products may be genetically modified and grown with high levels of chemicals, so use organic soya. Be aware that non-organic soya is also added to a lot of processed foods.

Soya that has been fermented (such as tempeh) is much healthier than non-fermented, as the fermentation process lessens the thyroid-lowering effect, and breaks down so-called 'anti nutrients' which prevent nutrients being metabolised.

If you are dairy-free, soya isn't the only vegan milk alternative. Why not try hemp milk, coconut milk, rice milk or almond milk?

UMEBOSHI PLUMS We say that 'an apple a day keeps the doctor away', but the Japanese put their faith in the umeboshi plum.

Umeboshi is a great digestive aid because it is both sour and salty. It acts as a tonic for the liver and kidneys due to its alkalising effect on the body, which also helps it to detox.

Umeboshi paste also has an antibacterial effect, so its use in sushi helps stop rice from spoiling. It's an important ingredient in sushi, in fact—working as a sort of edible glue that helps bind the roll together.

MISO paste is another fermented soya product. Like yoghurt it is a living fermented food, valued for its beneficial bacteria. Cooking destroys these healthy bugs so miso is added to soup after it has boiled and cooled slightly. There are many different types, but my favourite is mugi miso, which is made with barley and has a rich and sweet taste.

SEAWEED is really popular in Macrobiotic cooking. It contains a lot of nutrients, particularly iodine, which is not so common in everyday vegetables. Macrobiotic cooking also uses seaweed to complement soya products like tofu.

KOMBU is the large brown seaweed you often see sticking out of the water at low tide. The leaves are dried and sold in long strips. I just add a strip to rice or pulses as I am cooking them so the nutrients are absorbed into the food. If you don't like seaweed you can take it out like a bay leaf. If you leave it in the dish though, the sliminess of seaweed actually makes the pulses more digestible as it soothes the intestine.

NORI comes from leafy red seaweed that is formed into sheets. The sheets are popularly used to form sushi rolls, or they can be roasted for a tasty snack.

HIJIKI is a smaller brown seaweed that comes in strands. These quickly rehydrate in hot water, and are great added to salads and stir fries.

Sushi Nori Rolls

160 g short grain brown rice

400 ml water

1 tbsp rice vinegar

2 sheets sushi nori

1 **carrot** *cut into sticks & steamed*

1 **small red pepper** *cut into sticks*

½ **avocado** *peeled, destoned
& cut into long slices*

8 slices pickled ginger

1 tbsp tahini

1 tbsp umeboshi paste

½ tsp wasabi

½ **lemon** *juiced*

½ tsp sesame seeds

TO SERVE

30 ml tamari

Place the rice and water in a pan with a well-fitting lid. Bring to the boil, cover and simmer for 35 minutes. It should absorb all the liquid; if it dries out add a bit more water. The rice should be soft and slightly sticky. Let it cool.

Place a sheet of nori on a sushi mat. Mix the cooked rice with the rice vinegar. Spread half the rice on the nori, leaving a clear 1 cm border on the edge furthest from you.

Arrange half the vegetables, ginger slices and avocado along the centre of the sushi, parallel to the border.

Mix together the tahini, lemon juice, umeboshi paste and wasabi. Spoon half of the mix evenly over the vegetables.

Dry roast the sesame seeds in a pan and sprinkle half over the rice.

Picking up the bottom edge of the sushi mat, roll up towards the filling. Keep the vegetables in the middle, and press firmly onto the nori. Wet the last edge of nori and seal the roll, squeezing to get it tight.

Repeat with the second sheet. Chill for at least one hour. Cut into slices and serve with a little tamari.

HERBS & SPICES

Herbs and spices are more than simply taste enhancers. Most of them can really help you with digestion, while others are powerful medicines too.

I mention some of the benefits here, but please check with a medical herbalist before using concentrated amounts of herbs and spices for medicinal purposes.

As a general rule, reduce the amount of flavourings you use if you are pregnant.

ASAFOETIDA This very strong spice is used extensively in Indian food. The taste becomes milder when it is fried in oil or ghee—in much the same way that the flavour of onions and leeks softens during cooking. In fact, it's often used instead of onions or garlic.

Asafoetida's beneficial effect on intestinal flora means it's commonly used in lentil dishes to help reduce bloating.

CHILLI POWDER has a warming quality to it (although Ayurveda generally recommends using black pepper rather than chilli as a warming spice). Chilli increases the appetite and circulation, and can be used instead of coffee to keep you awake! (Also see Chilli Peppers page 171.)

CUMIN is a key spice in Indian and Middle Eastern cooking. The seeds are normally fried in hot oil (until they pop) or used in powdered form. In Sanskrit it is called jeera which literally means 'that which helps digestion'.

GINGER is used fresh, dried or ground in savoury and sweet dishes. It is of course the main ingredient in chai (Indian spiced tea). It is warming, so it stimulates digestion. It also reduces nausea and is good for travel sickness. It is used extensively in Ayurvedic cooking.

LOVAGE is a wonderful herb to grow in your garden because it comes up and gets bigger every year. Its leaves are delicious and really bring any soup to life. The seeds can be used as a spice and the roots are edible too.

CHINESE FIVE SPICE This is a mixture of spices containing star anise, cloves, cinnamon, pepper and fennel seeds. Star anise is a Chinese star-shaped fruit with a similar taste to aniseed.

CURRY POWDER is a Western invention resulting from the popularisation of Indian food. There is no fixed recipe; it is a blend of Indian spices used during cooking. It normally contains: coriander, turmeric, cumin and fenugreek, but may also include ginger, garlic, fennel, cinnamon, clove, mustard seed, cardamom or black pepper. It's useful if you just want a quick mix of spices.

My Six Taste Spice Mix is a sort of curry powder but based on Ayurvedic principles of health and sprinkled on the food after it is served.

FENNEL originated in the Mediterranean regions but due to its popular use has spread to many parts of the world as a wild plant. The bulbs can be eaten as a vegetable, raw or braised. The fresh or dried leaves are used as a herb.

The seeds are popular and have a calming effect on the digestion. In India, fennel seeds are chewed after a meal to help digestion.

FENUGREEK has been cultivated for many thousands of years. It is used as a seed and ground powder, a dried herb from the leaves and also as a vegetable. It has a reputation as an effective galactagogue—increasing the breast milk in lactating mothers. It is also used as a herbal medicine to help control diabetes.

GARAM MASALA This is a more authentic Indian spice mix than curry powder. It is not a totally fixed recipe, but typically contains peppercorns, cloves, cinnamon, cumin seeds and cardamom seeds.

CORIANDER The entire coriander plant is edible. Leaves are commonly used as a garnish and an ingredient in Indian cooking. The seeds have a lemony flavour and are usually ground and used as a spice.

CLOVES Native to Indonesia, cloves are the buds of the clove tree, used widely as a sweet, but warm, spice. Clove essential oil has anaesthetic properties and is often used to numb toothache.

MIXED HERBS This blend typically contains marjoram, thyme, basil and oregano. It's convenient and quick, and saves you having to reach for individual herbs. Saves space in your cupboard too.

BLACK MUSTARD SEEDS I use black mustard seeds a lot. I heat them in oil and they pop like popcorn. Keep your face away from the pan and cover the pan with a lid as they go everywhere!

Jesus likened this seed to faith, as the seeds are small but they grow into large plants. It also spreads and can end up everywhere (so some might even regard as a weed and try to root it out).

Buddha also used the mustard seed in his teachings. A grieving mother once brought her dead child to him to bring back to life. The Buddha asked her to bring him a mustard seed from a family house where no-one had died. Of course she could not, thus demonstrating that death and grief are part of life.

PARSLEY, SAGE, ROSEMARY & THYME

The names of these four herbs bring a certain Simon and Garfunkel melody to mind. 'Scarborough Fair' is in fact a very old folk song dating back to the 1600s. It developed from an even older Celtic love song, in which a lover lists a series of impossible tasks for his beloved to perform in order to gain true love. Parsley, sage, rosemary and thyme are included for their unique qualities. The herbs had a language of their own and infused the song with a hidden meaning. The lyrics said one thing, but the coded message in the herbs said another.

Parsley was a herb used to remove bitterness from a meal. So, in mentioning parsley the singer is promising to remove any bitterness from their pasts in order to clear the way for new love. Sage was thought to give strength and health. So here the chorus means 'let us enjoy health and happiness together'. Rosemary was present in the wedding bouquet as a symbol of love and fidelity. Its fragrance lingers and does not fade easily, so it promises a love that will last forever. Finally thyme represents courage. It was offered as such to gallant knights by admiring ladies. Courage comes from the French word cœur, meaning 'heart'. So, to give thyme means 'let us follow our hearts, take courage and spend thyme together'.

The four herbs together were used as a love potion in the Middle Ages and in the Four Thieves Vinegar (page 173).

PARSLEY When I grew up, parsley was just an attractive herb used as a garnish, a sprig to brighten up colourless dishes such as mashed potato. But this understates this versatile herb. Parsley is not just a pretty face, it's also a highly nutritious superfood. It is packed with vitamins, minerals and is also full of flavour. A popular medicinal herb, parsley is traditionally used as a diuretic and mild kidney tonic.

SAGE is another wonderful herb to have in your garden, as it grows easily into an abundant flowering bush. It's not just delicious in cooking but also acts as a digestive aid. Sage leaves are a popular 'women's tea' and thought to help reduce menopausal symptoms. It is also credited with antiseptic qualities.

ROSEMARY, like sage, is a wonderful addition to your garden as it is very decorative and useful. It grows into a hardy, drought-resistant bush. The flowers were said to have been white until biblical times. When Mother Mary placed her blue cloak over the plant as she rested, the flowers turned blue and it has been called rosemary ever since—the 'rose of Mary'.

Not only is rosemary popular in Mediterranean dishes and traditional British cooking, it also has many health benefits. It's thought to stimulate hair growth and is traditionally used as a natural conditioner for brown hair. It's also credited with improving memory and as such it is associated with remembrance, particularly in Australia and New Zealand where a sprig of rosemary is worn on Anzac Day.

THYME is a resilient little garden herb that will spread and grow year after year. Originating in Eastern Mediterranean regions, it spread throughout Europe with the Romans. It is an aromatic herb and not only imparts a delicious flavour but also helps digestion. Thyme is a noted medicinal herb; thymol extracted from the leaves is still used as an antibiotic in commercial mouthwash.

NUTMEG Originating in Indonesia, nutmeg is the fruit of an evergreen tree. I think of it as a 2-in-1 spice—the nutmeg is surrounded by 'mace', which is a bit milder. I use nutmeg in both sweet and savoury dishes.

PAPRIKA looks like, and is related to, chilli powder but is much milder and sweeter. Paprika is great to use in many dishes as it adds colour, sweetness and a little bit of spice. The hotness varies and you can also get smoked paprika. It is most famous though for being the main ingredient in Samia's Spice Mix (page 278).

SUMMER SAVORY I first came across this in Bulgarian cookery. It is a great little herb and is slightly milder than sage.

OREGANO Originally from Southern Europe, it is aromatic and has a stronger flavour when dried. However, the varieties suited to cooler climates tend to have a less intense flavour.

MANGO POWDER You would expect mango powder to be very sweet but, as it's made from the dried slices of unripe green mango, it's actually quite sour and tart. It's used in North Indian cooking and in my Six Taste Spice Mix (page 270).

TURMERIC As bright colours in food indicate the presence of antioxidants, it's no surprise that the most vibrantly coloured of spices, turmeric, is packed with them. Not only does turmeric add a golden richness to food, it also abounds in healthy nutrients.

It seems like every day new research ascribes yet more health benefits to this colourful spice. Turmeric is high in curcumin which is a powerful anti-inflammatory and antioxidant. Turmeric is also thought to help lift your mood, which may become necessary when it stains your clothes, worktops and carpets if you are not careful.

Turmeric is tremendously good for your health

ESSENTIAL
ORGANIC
Raw
Virgin
Coconut Oil
granoVita
Organic
Flax Oil
Rich in Omega-3
Virgin Cold Pressed
pukka

MY FAVOURITE FATS & OILS

COCONUT OIL Highly nutritious, coconut oil is rich in the healthy, shorter length fatty acids—making it easy to digest.

Coconut oil, like ghee, activates our digestive system to burn up unwanted fats and toxins. A sluggish digestive system combined with a faulty diet will leave a lot of toxic residue in the body in the form of undigested food. Consider how a fire fuelled with damp wood will not burn completely. We need to add the right kind of fuel to get the fire going. In our case, foods like coconut oil or ghee can boost our digestive fire.

In the 1940s, farmers tried using coconut oil as a potentially cheap food to fatten their animals. They soon discovered that it made them lean and active instead, and also increased their appetites! Great for the animals' health, but not so good for profits. They switched to soya beans, which proved much more cost effective. The soya lowered the animals' thyroid function, so they became less active, gained more weight, and at the same time reduced their appetites.

However, as most of us are not trying to fatten ourselves up at a minimal cost, why not use coconut oil rather than soya or corn oil for your home cooking? It's important to choose unrefined 'virgin' cold pressed coconut oil, stored in glass (not plastic). It may cost more, but a little goes a long way.

About 50% of coconut oil is in the form of a fat called lauric acid. This is not only a good energy source, but it also has a healthy anti-bacterial effect. Lauric acid in the body is converted into monolaurin, which disrupts the membranes of (and destroys) such organisms as fungus, bacteria and viruses. Coconut oil also contains about 10% caprylic acid, which is another rapidly metabolised oil with a powerful anti-fungal effect that can help reduce candida.

In India, coconut oil is widely used as a hair oil. This is great in a hot country, but it sets hard at low temperatures, so in a British winter you may find your hair goes a bit solid! It's fantastic for your skin, and makes a great massage oil. Coconut oil is anti-bacterial and can also be used for 'oil pulling'—the Ayurvedic way to clean your teeth. A little oil is placed in the mouth and you swish it between your teeth for a few minutes before spitting it out.

GHEE In Ayurveda, ghee is regarded as something really special—the finest essence of milk, which is itself pure and sacred. I consider ghee to be one of my essential superfoods.

Rich and golden in colour, ghee is thought to reflect the radiance of the sun. To me, ghee is solar energy in a jar!

The sun's rays are first captured by the chlorophyll in the green grass, the ideal diet of cows. The tough cellulose in the leaves is then transformed by the cows into milk. The best of the milk is taken off as cream, which is then made into butter. Finally the butterfat is purified to create ghee.

Some people who are normally allergic to dairy products (lactose intolerant) can use ghee because all the milk solids have been removed. This means you can get the buttery taste without the allergies. At last! You really can have your cake and eat it—as long as it's made with ghee instead of butter. The absence of milk solids means it keeps better than butter and doesn't need to be refrigerated. Simply store in a sealed container, away from direct sunlight.

I cook mainly with either ghee or coconut oil—both are saturated fats and therefore more heat stable. When heated, other oils break down into harmful free radicals which can damage your cells.

Ghee is a nutritious food (unlike refined or processed oils) and contains natural anti-oxidants and vitamins, especially if the cows were grass-fed. Milk fat from grass-fed cows contains higher amounts of the much needed omega-3 essential fatty acids, as well as other nutrients.

Amazingly, ghee is the fat that can actually help you lose weight! Unlike other animal fats, it has a number of short chain fatty acids, which gives it the buttery taste and metabolises easily into energy—a bit like carbohydrates. This metabolic process helps your body burn up other fats at the same time.

In Ayurveda, ghee is thought to increase the 'digestive fire' and strengthen digestion. It's used as a medicine to detox the system. Medicated ghee is used to draw out toxins stored in other fats in the body. Ghee is also considered to be soothing for the intestines.

Ghee is referred to in a popular Hindu verse known as the 'Brahma Prayer' which is traditionally recited before eating.

Brahman is a Sanskrit word meaning 'oneness' or 'that which exists beyond form'. It's actually what physicists are looking for—the source of everything. It's the ultimate principle from which all things are formed.

We might think that 'beyond form' is emptiness like outer space. But mystics say beyond form is fullness, bliss and pure awareness, and that the closest emotion or feeling we have to this is love.

Brahmar panam Brahma havir

Brahma gnau Brahma naahutam

Brahmaiva tena Ghantavyam

Brahma karma Samadhina

The act of offering is Brahman

What is offered is Brahman

Brahman offers the sacrifice into the fire of Brahman

He who sees Brahman in every action attains Brahman

Bhagavad Gita

Chapter 4, verse 24

The 'Brahma Prayer' is used at mealtimes as it is symbolic of eating food.

It says the act of offering (eating) is oneness, and so is the food. The fire (digestion) is also oneness and so are we. It concludes that the person who is aware of this in every action enters into this bliss, or self awareness.

It is quite a philosophical concept but to intellectualise it too much would miss the point.

In essence it is saying the same thing as this book's title: 'Cooking with Love' is one of the best ways to bring joy and unity into our lives.

Ghee

Ghee is made by melting butter to separate the fat from the milk solids and water content. Traditionally ghee is simmered for 10 minutes to remove any residual water and caramelise it slightly. This gives it its distinctive nutty taste.

250 g unsalted butter
organic and from grass-fed cows if possible

Dice the butter and place in a saucepan. Heat until the butter has completely melted. Reduce the heat and simmer gently.

The butter will separate into three layers: a sediment at the bottom, a foam at the top, and the ghee in the middle.

At first there is a lot of steam as the liquid part of the butter is boiled away. Continue simmering for about 5–10 minutes.

The ghee is ready when there is less steam and the sediment at the bottom starts to go brown. Remove from the heat and skim off the foam with a spoon or strainer. Allow it to cool slightly.

While it is still runny, carefully decant the ghee into a clean container, leaving the sediment in the bottom of the pan.

Cover and store at room temperature.

It stays fresh for 1–2 weeks.

Keith's safety tip Do not leave the pan unattended on the stove as you are making the ghee.

HEMP OIL is high in omega-3 essential fatty acids and needs to be stored in a dark bottle in the fridge.

Hemp oil's ratio of omega-6 to omega-3 fats is very close to the optimum balance our body needs. This means hemp oil can be used continuously without causing an imbalance in essential fatty acids. Hemp also provides GLA—a more advanced form of omega-6 known to help balance hormones and improve mood swings. (GLA is commonly sought in the form of Evening Primrose supplements or Borage oil.)

I never cook with hemp oil but use it in dips or as a salad dressing. You can use it as a sauce by simply pouring it over your meal—even a small amount can lubricate your food and make it easier to digest. An excellent way to get really fresh hemp oil is to eat hemp seeds, which are nearly 50% fat anyway. I simply grind a handful and sprinkle them over my food.

LINSEED OIL is probably best known as a natural varnish for treating wood. It soaks into the wood, allowing it to 'breathe' and preserving its natural look.

The good news is that linseed oil can help keep us naturally healthy too, due to its high concentration of omega-3. Most of us have far too much omega-6 in our diet, so we need lots of omega-3 to compensate (read 'Fats & Oils' page 68). Taking linseed oil is a good way to correct this imbalance as it contains over 50% omega-3. (Some fats, such as soya oil and corn oil, are deficient in omega-3 but unfortunately are commonly used in processed foods.)

The only disadvantage of linseed oil is that it can go off quickly, thereby losing a lot of its beneficial qualities. It's important to check that the oil is fresh to begin with, then to store it in a cool place away from strong light. Linseed oil is therefore best stored in a dark, airtight container in the fridge. Try to use it up within a few weeks of opening. It should have a sweet, nutty smell. If it doesn't, throw it out (or use it to varnish some wood).

Potatoes & Quark with Linseeds

Serves 4

500 g salad potatoes

1 tsp caraway seeds

150 ml quark or kefir

1 tbsp minced parsley

2 tbsp single cream

1 tsp linseed oil

1 tsp linseeds *freshly ground*

¼ tsp salt

pinch of pepper *to taste*

Cover the potatoes with water, add the caraway seeds and bring to the boil. Reduce the heat, cover with a lid and simmer for 15–20 minutes until the potatoes are tender. Then drain.

In a medium bowl, mix together the quark/kefir, parsley, cream, linseed oil, salt and pepper.
Add the warm potatoes.

Sprinkle with the freshly ground linseeds.

SESAME OIL While olive oil was popular in the Mediterranean region, sesame was the favourite oil of the Orient. Originally it came from northern India, and was used as long as 5,000 years ago. Sesame is popular as it is a nutritious, drought-resistant crop. Sesame's high concentration of natural anti-oxidants helps to keep it fresh longer than most oils.

Toasted sesame oil is popular in Asian cooking. I sometimes use it to give a traditional nutty taste to stir fries. However, as it is a polyunsaturated fat, sesame is most nutritious when cold pressed and raw. For this reason I prefer to sprinkle some cold pressed sesame oil over food after cooking. Though not quite as strong tasting as the toasted oil, it still adds its distinctive flavour.

Sesame oil has a long history as a cosmetic. It is rich in minerals including zinc and calcium so it is nourishing for skin and hair. Like olive oil, it has natural antioxidant and anti-inflammatory effects. Sesame's health qualities make sesame oil popular in Ayurvedic medicine where it's used as a massage and hair oil. Like coconut it can also be employed in 'oil pulling', the Ayurvedic tooth cleaning method.

EXTRA VIRGIN OLIVE OIL

There is evidence that olive oil was made as early as 6,000 BC. Olive trees have been cultivated for so long it is not clear where they originally came from, but it's thought to be either modern day Greece or Turkey. By 200 BC, the trade in olive oil was well established in Mediterranean countries and the oil was commonly used in ancient Greek and Roman cuisine.

I prefer to cook with coconut oil or ghee generally, but sometimes use olive oil to lightly cook vegetables if the temperature doesn't need to get too high.

Olive oil is mainly oleic acid, which is a mono-saturated fatty acid and therefore slightly more heat-stable than polyunsaturated oils.

I always use cold pressed, extra virgin olive oil. Other types, even those labelled 'pure olive oil' are still refined. As the fatty acids can get damaged on heating, olive oil (like most oils) is best eaten raw. Get freshly made, excellent quality oils whenever you can—they are richer in nutrients and taste far better too.

Olive oil, a popular ingredient in Mediterranean cooking, is thought to be good for your heart. This is partly because the oleic acid can have a beneficial effect on cholesterol. There are lots of natural antioxidants and anti-inflammatory nutrients in olive oil. These may also help protect you from heart disease and other chronic illness.

Olive oil has a long history as a cosmetic too. In ancient Egypt it was used as a skin moisturiser and conditioner. The ancient Romans used it as a body oil because its anti-inflammatory qualities make it a soothing massage oil and the antioxidants and other nutrients detox and nourish the skin.

From the primordial soup*
that sustained the first life
on our planet, to the cream
of tomato today, soups
nourish and satisfy like no
other meal.

*recipe not supplied

Soups

Cooking vegetables slowly in water is one of the most ancient ways of preparing food. It all started by taking hot rocks from the fire and placing them into water with forest foods (to make them edible). We've come a long way since then. But still, eating a warming soup whilst sitting by the fire has a magic that evokes timeless emotions.

Vegetarian soups combine ingredients such as beans, grains and vegetables with stock, or flavoured liquid. They can be a clear soup, called bouillon, or a thick soup which has been thickened with cream, flour, lentils or potatoes. Thick soups can also be made by blending cooked vegetables into a purée.

Soups are easy to digest, particularly when herbs and spices like ginger or pepper are added. Some of the recipes here include pulses, which provide additional protein. When eaten with healthy bread made from wholegrain flour, a soup can be a meal in itself.

A tasty vegetable stock is the foundation for all good soups. Adding just water can dilute the taste, so you can end up adding too much salt to compensate. Stock on the other hand adds a depth of flavour and contains natural salts from vegetables. If you decide to use a ready-made stock, choose a good quality one made from natural ingredients. I find that the Marigold range of bouillon powders is really good, or you can make your own (see page 181).

When I am cooking a soup with pulses, such as mung beans or lentils, I start off by cooking them with some stock powder. To this, I add finely chopped onion, celery, carrot, bay leaf and a few peppercorns. This builds the flavour during the long cooking time and these ingredients almost completely dissolve. I add the other vegetables and herbs later, to add texture, colour and flavour to the dish.

Real Welsh Leek & Potato Soup

Leeks are a symbol of Wales and potatoes are the
nation's favourite food. Together they make
a wonderful winter warmer.

Serves 4–6

1 tbsp butter or coconut oil

1 onion *sliced*

225 g potatoes *peeled & diced*

2 medium leeks *sliced*

1,200 ml vegetable stock

¼ tsp ground black pepper

1 tsp lovage leaves *chopped*
(optional)

150 ml double cream

1 tbsp chopped fresh parsley

Heat the butter/coconut oil in a large pan and add the
prepared onion, potatoes and leeks. Sauté for
3–4 minutes until the vegetables start to soften.

Pour the vegetable stock into the pan and bring to the
boil. Season with black pepper and lovage (if available).

Simmer for about 20 minutes until the vegetables
are tender.

You can keep the soup in this consistency or liquidise it in
a food processor or by using a stick blender. If you choose
to do the latter, you may need to reheat it in a clean pan.

Before serving, stir in the cream and garnish with
chopped fresh parsley.

Carrot & Coriander Soup

This version of the popular soup uses both ground coriander and fresh coriander leaves, each quite different in taste. This soup becomes extra fragrant if you grind your own coriander seeds. Before grinding, dry roast them in a frying pan on a low heat for a few minutes until they smell fragrant—being careful not to burn them.

Serves 2-3

1 tbsp ghee or coconut oil

1 onion finely *chopped*

½ tsp ground coriander

1 celery stick *sliced*

250 g carrots *peeled & sliced*

2 small potatoes *peeled & chopped*

500 ml vegetable stock

1 tbsp chopped fresh coriander

75 ml single cream

salt & pepper

Heat the ghee/coconut oil in a large saucepan. Fry the onion over a gentle heat for 3–4 minutes, until slightly softened but not browned.

Stir in the coriander powder. Add the celery, carrots and potato and cook for a few minutes.

Reduce the heat, cover the pan and let the vegetables stew in their own steam for about 5 minutes. Stir occasionally so the vegetables do not stick to the pan.

Add the stock, bring to the boil, cover and simmer until all the vegetables are tender.

Liquidise the soup in a food processor or using a stick blender (add more stock if it is too thick).

Reheat the soup gently, then stir in the cream and fresh coriander. Season to taste with salt and pepper.

Vegetable Minestrone

Minestrone is a rustic Italian dish and is not a set recipe. It refers to a thick soup made from available vegetables. In Latin 'fruges' originally referred to the common food made from cereals, vegetables and pulses. Minestrone was considered a frugal food and yet always recognised as a healthy way of eating.

Serves 4-6

1 medium potato *peeled & diced*

2 sticks celery *sliced*

1 carrot *diced*

100 g swede *peeled & diced*

100 g cabbage or kale *sliced*

1 medium leek *sliced*

1 onion *sliced*

2 garlic cloves *crushed*

2 tbsp extra virgin olive oil

1¾ ltr vegetable stock

2 medium courgettes *diced*

400 g tin butter beans *drained & rinsed*

1 tbsp chopped fresh parsley

1 tsp lovage leaves *chopped (optional)*

1 tbsp chopped fresh basil

salt & pepper *to taste*

Leaving aside the courgettes, sauté the other vegetables and garlic in olive oil, with about 3 tablespoons of water.

Stir and cook for 5 minutes over a medium heat.

Cover with stock and bring to the boil.

Simmer for about 10 minutes or until the vegetables are tender. Add the courgettes along with the beans, lovage and parsley. Bring back to the boil and then lower the heat and simmer for 5 minutes.

Season to taste with salt and pepper.

Add the basil just before serving.

Indian Dhal & Carrot

Dhal is a generic Ayurvedic term for soupy dishes made from pulses. It's the main protein dish in India and the exact recipe varies from place to place. Dhal translated means 'split', as it is normally made from halved pulses like red lentils. To help make them more digestible, these are cooked for a long time with plenty of water. You can use an off-the-shelf garam masala or make your own using my recipe on page 280.

Serves 4

2 tbsp coconut oil or ghee

1 medium onion *coarsely chopped*

3 garlic cloves *crushed*

½ tsp ground cumin

½ tsp ground turmeric

1 tsp ground coriander

2 tsp ground paprika

1 tsp garam masala

1 medium carrot *diced*

1 medium potato *peeled & diced*

750 ml vegetable stock

150 g red lentils *washed*

1 tbsp chopped fresh coriander

Heat the coconut oil/ghee in a pan and cook the onion and garlic until soft.

Over a very low heat, stir in the ground cumin, turmeric, paprika, coriander and garam masala. Continue cooking for about 30 seconds until it gives off a sweet fragrance.

Add the carrot and sauté for a few more minutes.

Stir in the stock, potato and lentils.

Bring to the boil and then simmer for 30 minutes. You may need to skim any froth off the top. Add more stock if it dries out too much.

Garnish with fresh coriander.

Clear Spring Vegetable Soup

This soup is great for the warmer times of year and you can use any seasonal vegetables. Quinoa is a very healthy addition. It not only adds nutrients and protein, but it's also alkaline-forming in the body—which makes it a perfect ingredient for a spring detox.

Serves 4

2 tsp butter or coconut oil

1 medium onion *chopped*

2 garlic cloves *crushed*

1 leek *sliced*

1 carrot *sliced*

1 celery stick *sliced*

100 g mushrooms *chopped*

1 ltr vegetable stock

50 g quinoa *rinsed*

1 tbsp chopped fresh parsley

salt & pepper *to taste*

Heat the butter/coconut oil in large pan and gently cook the onion and garlic until soft.

Add the leek, carrot and celery and continue cooking and stirring until tender.

Add the mushrooms and cook for one more minute.

Stir in the stock and quinoa; bring to the boil and then simmer for 15 minutes.

Stir in the parsley, season to taste and serve.

Butternut Squash Soup

This soup contains two of my favourite vegetables: sweet potatoes and butternut squash. Both are substantial, delicious and an ideal base for any vegetarian dish.

Serves 4-6

1 tbsp ghee or coconut oil

½ tsp cumin seeds

½ tsp ground turmeric

1 bay leaf

1 leek *sliced*

500 g butternut squash *peeled & chopped*

500 g sweet potato *peeled & chopped*

1 ltr vegetable stock

1 tsp grated fresh ginger

salt & pepper *to taste*

Heat the ghee/coconut oil in a pan and add the cumin seeds. Allow them to roast for a few seconds.

When they smell fragrant add the turmeric, bay leaf and leek. Stir for a minute or two.

Add the other vegetables, ginger and stock, bring to the boil and then simmer for 35 minutes. Remove the bay leaf, then liquidise in a food processor or using a stick blender.

Season with salt and pepper, and serve.

Misoshiru
Traditional Miso Soup

This is the Macrobiotic answer to the iconic British Bovril Soup! Miso is not only nourishing but has a detoxifying effect on the body. Like yoghurt, it has beneficial bacteria which help improve digestion. To preserve this probiotic effect, the miso is dissolved and stirred into the soup after it has finished cooking and been removed from the heat. The tofu and vegetables add substance to the soup and the seaweed adds extra minerals.

Serves 4

2 cm strip kombu seaweed

2 spring onions *finely sliced*

100 g broccoli *cut into small florets*

1 carrot *cut into small dice*

1 tsp grated fresh ginger

1 ltr vegetable stock

1 tbsp arame seaweed

200 g tofu *cut into small dice*

100 ml brown rice miso or barley miso

1 tbsp chopped fresh parsley

Mix the kombu, ginger, broccoli, carrot and spring onions with the stock. Bring to the boil and simmer for 15 minutes.

Add the tofu and arame. Simmer for a further 5 minutes and remove from the heat.

The kombu strip can now be removed.

Ladle some of the soup into a separate bowl and dissolve the miso paste into it.

Pour the miso mixture back into the soup.

Serve while it is still warm and garnish with fresh parsley.

Spinach Soup

This soup is bright green so it must be good! I like to swirl cream
into the finished soup for a wonderful effect.

Serves 2-3

50 g butter or coconut oil

1 medium onion *finely chopped*

2 garlic cloves *finely chopped*

1 medium potato *peeled & diced*

400 ml vegetable stock

200 g spinach *chopped*

100 ml cream

salt & pepper *to taste*

Melt the butter/coconut oil and sauté the onion and garlic for a few minutes.

Add the potato and cook for another couple of minutes.

Add the stock and bring to the boil.

Cover and simmer for 10 minutes, or until the potato is soft.

Stir in the spinach and reheat over a low heat for about 5 minutes.

Liquidise in a food processor or using a stick blender.

Add the cream and season with salt and pepper.

Cashew & Ginger Soup

Cashews can be used to thicken soups and sauces as they contain more starch than other nuts. The apple and vegetables add a natural sweetness to this refreshing but satisfying soup.

Serves 4-6

1 onion *sliced*

50 g butter or coconut oil

1 small sweet potato *peeled & chopped*

1 small apple *grated*

1 celery stick *finely sliced*

1 small potato *diced*

1 ltr vegetable stock

½ tsp grated fresh ginger

50 g cashew nuts *roughly chopped*

1 tbsp chopped fresh chives

salt & pepper *to taste*

Melt the butter/coconut oil and sauté the onion and celery till softened.

Add the sweet potato and apple and cook for a few minutes.

Add the stock, ginger, potato and cashews.

Bring to the boil, cover and simmer for about 20 minutes until the vegetables are tender.

Liquidise in a food processor or using a stick blender.

Season to taste.

Stir in the chives and serve.

Irish Stew with Dumplings

Another winter favourite. Again it is making the most of seasonal vegetables. I've used butter instead of suet in the dumplings because suet is either not vegetarian or, if vegetarian, prepared with refined fats. This stew is slow cooked in the oven but could also be made in a pan with a lid—which would reduce the cooking time.

FOR THE STEW

2 tbsp butter or coconut oil

2 garlic cloves *peeled & crushed*

1 medium onion *peeled & diced*

2 sticks celery *cut into large chunks*

2 carrots *cut into large chunks*

1 leek *roughly chopped*

200 g swede
peeled & cut into large chunks

750 ml vegetable stock

150 g red lentils *rinsed well*

2 bay leaves

3 tbsp chopped fresh thyme

3 tbsp chopped fresh flat leaf parsley

1 tbsp balsamic vinegar

salt & pepper *to taste*

FOR THE DUMPLINGS

125 g self-raising wholemeal flour

1 tsp baking powder

pinch of salt

50 g butter or coconut oil

about 60 ml water
enough to make a dough

Preheat the oven to 175°C.

Heat the butter/coconut oil in a large pan, sauté the garlic and all the vegetables for 1–2 minutes.

Stir in the vegetable stock, bay leaves, lentils and herbs, and reheat.

Add the balsamic vinegar and season with salt and freshly ground black pepper.

Transfer to a 2.5 litre oven-proof dish with a lid. Cover and bake in the oven for about two hours, or until the lentils are tender.

Meanwhile, make the dumplings by sifting the flour, baking powder and salt into a bowl. Rub in the butter/coconut oil, then add enough water to form a thick dough. With floured hands, roll spoonfuls of the dough into small balls.

After two hours, remove the lid from the stew and place the dumpling balls on top of the stew.

Cover, return to the oven and cook for a further 25 minutes, or until the dumplings have swollen and are tender.

Cream of Tomato Soup

As a child one of my favourite lunchtime meals was a tin of tomato soup eaten with toast. This recipe takes more effort but it's really worth it. To prepare the tomatoes, cover them in boiling water and allow to stand for 1 minute. Drain and then peel.

Serves 2-3

2 tbsp extra virgin olive oil

2 onions *chopped*

2 garlic cloves *crushed*

1 tsp dried oregano

½ tsp dried basil

½ tsp fennel seeds

1 medium sized courgette *diced*

50 g tomato purée

250 g fresh tomatoes *peeled & sliced*

250 ml vegetable stock

100 ml single cream

salt & pepper *to taste*

Heat the olive oil, and sauté the onion, garlic, fennel seeds and dried herbs for a few minutes.

Add the courgette, tomato purée, peeled tomatoes and stock, and bring to the boil. Simmer for 20 minutes.

Take off the heat and liquidise in a food processor or using a stick blender.

Add the cream and season to taste.

Creamy Courgette Soup

Serves 4

1 tbsp butter or coconut oil

1 onion *peeled & sliced*

2 garlic cloves *crushed*

½ tsp ground paprika

1 medium courgette *diced*

1 medium potato *peeled & diced*

650 ml vegetable stock

1 tbsp chopped fresh parsley

1 tbsp single cream

Heat the butter/coconut oil in a pan, add the onion and garlic, then stir for a few minutes.

Stir in the ground paprika and continue cooking for another minute.

Add the courgette and potato with the stock and bring to the boil.

Cover and simmer for about 15 minutes.

Liquidise in a food processor or using a stick blender.

Reheat. Add the cream and parsley and serve.

Salads

Fresh salads made with oil, herbs and lemon juice have been popular ever since ancient Roman and Greek times. In Britain, however, salads have historically been avoided, possibly due to hygiene and food safety concerns. They only caught on after the late 1800s when salads' popularity started to grow in the USA.

It feels natural to have at least a small amount of raw food with our cooked meal. It's almost as if our bodies crave a certain amount of the living food's inherent vitality and there's nothing better than crispy, vibrant fresh salad—especially in summer!

This vitality, also called prana, is thought to be abundant in nature: in trees, plants, moving water and fresh air. That's why we feel so energised by being outside. Practising yoga and pranayama outdoors in nature is much more powerful than doing it indoors because we draw on the natural vital energy around us.

Prana is also in food. It won't tell you that on the packet but perhaps it should! It is highest in fresh, living foods like fruits and vegetables, particularly those grown in the sunlight. Yogis describe it as stored solar energy. Seeds, nuts and grains are thought to store prana in order to create a new plant.

Instead of eating salad ingredients cold, straight out of the fridge, I often wash them in warm water, leave them to reach room temperature or use a heated dressing. Ayurveda recommends that raw foods and salads should be warmed with dressings to help make them more digestible. The sour taste of lemon and vinegar, the salt, and the warming spices all work to stimulate digestion.

In the following pages, I recommend kefir as a salad ingredient. Kefir is similar to yoghurt but contains more beneficial bacteria. They replace less beneficial ones in the digestive tract. Kefir also tends to be slightly more sour and runny than yoghurt. If you can't find kefir, you can use live natural yoghurt.

Keith's Ayurvedic Carrot Salad

Raw food, although full of vitality and living enzymes, can seem cold and unappetising. In Ayurvedic cooking there are warm salads which mix hot and cold ingredients, or have seasonings in the dressing that make them more digestible.

Serves 2-3

150 g carrots *peeled & grated*

100 g fennel bulb *finely sliced*

2 tbsp raisins

good pinch of salt

¼ tsp freshly ground black pepper

2 tsp chopped fresh parsley

1 tsp grated fresh ginger

2 tsp lemon juice

2 tbsp ghee or coconut oil

½ tsp black or brown mustard seed

pinch of asafoetida

1 tsp ground cumin

For this recipe you need a pan with a well-fitting lid.

Combine the carrots, fennel, raisins, salt, pepper, parsley and lemon juice in a bowl.

In the pan, gently melt the ghee/coconut oil.

Carefully add the mustard seeds, keeping your face away from the pan.

Cover with the lid, heat and wait for the seeds to pop. Remove from the heat and wait for the seeds to stop crackling. Still keeping your face away from the pan, carefully add the ginger, asafoetida and ground cumin. Let it sizzle for a few seconds.

Pour onto the salad. Mix well.

Quinoa Tabbouleh

A traditional tabbouleh would be made from bulgur wheat or couscous. In this version I have used quinoa as it is gluten free and higher in protein. You can vary the vegetables and herbs in the salad. I often include spring onions, baby spinach leaves or celery.

Serves 4

200 g quinoa *washed*

450 ml vegetable stock

1 tbsp hemp oil or linseed oil

2 tbsp extra virgin olive oil

2 tbsp tamari

2 tbsp lemon juice

2 garlic cloves *crushed*

1 red pepper *diced*

1 fennel bulb *finely sliced*

3 tbsp chopped fresh parsley

Place the quinoa in a medium pan and cover with the stock. Bring to the boil then reduce the heat and cover with a lid.

Simmer until the quinoa is cooked. (The grains are cooked when they are still a bit crunchy; there should be a dot of the original colour at the centre of the grain, like the pupil in an eye. This usually takes about 15 minutes.)

Drain off any excess water and fluff it up using a fork so the grains separate.

Transfer to a large salad bowl. Then add the oils, tamari, lemon juice and crushed garlic.

Finally, add the pepper, fennel and parsley, and toss to combine.

'Cool as a Cucumber' Raita

Raita is a generic term for dishes of raw or cooked vegetables mixed with yoghurt (although in this recipe you can also use kefir). Spices are added and normally 'tempered' or heated to release their flavour and essential oils into the dish. The most popular version of raita is with cucumber—a wonderful cooling salad on a hot summer's day.

Serves 2-3

1 cucumber *grated*

½ tsp cumin seeds

250 g ricotta cheese

100 ml kefir or live natural yoghurt

pinch of chilli powder

½ tsp ground coriander

¼ tsp wholegrain mustard

1 tbsp chopped fresh coriander

1 tbsp chopped fresh mint

salt *to taste*

Place the grated cucumber in a muslin cloth and squeeze out the excess water.

Meanwhile dry roast the cumin seeds in a pan until fragrant.

Whisk together the ricotta cheese and kefir/yoghurt, then add the roasted seeds. Stir in the powdered spices, herbs, mustard and salt.

Add the grated cucumber and mint.

Combine all ingredients together.

Garnish with the fresh coriander and serve.

Cucumber 'Squared' Salad

This is called cucumber 'squared' because there is a double helping of this vegetable, both in the salad and the dressing. Therefore you will need a whole cucumber and bunch of fresh basil.

Serves 3-4

DRESSING

100 g cucumber *roughly chopped*

50 ml kefir or live natural yoghurt

1 tbsp lemon juice

½ tbsp tahini

1 handful fresh basil *chopped*

¼ tsp salt

pinch pepper *to taste*

SALAD

280 g cucumber *peeled & sliced*

1 handful fresh basil *chopped*

For the dressing, put the cucumber chunks, kefir/yoghurt, lemon juice, tahini and basil into a food processor and blend until smooth.

Season with the salt and pepper.

For the salad, arrange the cucumber and basil in a bowl.

Pour the dressing over the salad and serve.

'BLT'

Beetroot, Lemon & Tamari

This salad not only looks stunning but is also very nutritious. The purple colour is due to the betacyanin in beetroot, which is a powerful antioxidant. The leaves of beetroot can also be eaten like spinach. You can add spring onions, baby spinach leaves or celery to this salad.

Serves 4

1 medium raw beetroot *peeled & grated*

1 carrot *peeled & grated*

1 small apple *grated*

2 tbsp chopped fresh parsley

1 tbsp chopped fresh chives

1 lemon

1 tsp tamari

1 tsp raw honey

1 tbsp hemp or linseed oil

salt & pepper *to taste*

Mix the fresh herbs with the grated vegetables and apple.

Using a fine grater, remove the rind from the lemon.

Mix the lemon rind into the salad, then stir in the tamari, honey and oil.

Squeeze 1 tablespoon of juice from the remainder of the lemon and mix it into the salad.

Season with salt and pepper.

Bavarian Potato

We get a lot of visitors from Germany who share their recipes with me—this being one! I originally made this with mayonnaise which I then changed to yoghurt for a healthier alternative. I now use kefir whenever I can for its probiotic benefits.

Serves 2-3

500 g new potatoes

2 tbsp chopped fresh dill or fresh chives

100 ml thick live yoghurt or kefir

3 pickled dill cucumbers *sliced*

1 tbsp spiced vinegar *from the dill cucumbers*

Cook the potatoes, allow them to cool and then chop into bite-size chunks.

Mix the cucumbers and fresh herbs through the potatoes—taking care not to break up the potatoes as you stir.

Whisk the vinegar into the yoghurt or kefir.

Dress the potatoes and serve.

Bulgarian Shopska

I discovered this dish while in Bulgaria.
It uses fresh sun-ripened tomatoes, soft salty
cheese and fresh herbs.

Serves 2-3

2 spring onions *finely chopped*

3 tomatoes *cut into bite-size chunks*

2 tbsp fresh parsley *chopped*

50 g feta or Bulgarian soft cheese
cut into chunks

½ cucumber *cut into large dice*

30 ml extra virgin olive oil

1 tsp chopped fresh oregano

Mix together the vegetables, herbs and cheese.

Dress with olive oil.

Millet Salad with Sunflower Seeds

This is like a Moroccan-style couscous but with millet as a healthy and wheat-free alternative to typical Moroccan couscous.

Serves 2-3

2 tbsp orange juice

50 g dried figs *finely chopped*

200 g millet

500 ml vegetable stock

4 tbsp sunflower seeds

1 tsp cumin seeds

2 tbsp tamari

2 tbsp extra virgin olive oil

1 tbsp hemp oil

2 spring onions *finely sliced*

small bunch chives *chopped*

Soak the figs in the orange juice and set aside while you prepare the rest of the salad.

Wash the millet carefully, place in a pan and add the stock.

Bring to the boil, then cover and simmer for about 20 minutes, or until the grains are just cooked.

Drain off any excess water and place the pan to one side.

Toast the cumin and sunflower seeds in a fresh dry pan until fragrant; keep them moving in the pan so that they don't burn.

Add the toasted seeds to the drained millet.

Stir in the oils and tamari. Add the chives, spring onions, soaked figs and any excess juice.

Transfer to a serving dish and serve.

Insalata Squires

Insalata comes from the Latin 'sal', which means salt, so it originally referred to a salted dish. In Italy it now means any salad dish with salt, oil and lemon, the simplest being 'insalataverde' or green salad. This 'Squires' variation includes my favourite salad vegetables.

Serves 2-3

1 ripe avocado *peeled & sliced*

2 tbsp lemon juice

250 g tomatoes *sliced into rings*

200 g mozzarella cheese *sliced*

3 spring onions *sliced*

75 g fresh basil *chopped*

100 g black pitted olives *drained & halved*

4 tbsp extra virgin olive oil

2 tbsp balsamic vinegar

salt & pepper

Place the avocado on a plate and pour the lemon juice over it to prevent discolouration.

Take one third of the avocado and place in a large glass salad bowl along with a third each of the tomato, cheese, onions, basil and olives.

Season with salt and pepper and a third of the olive oil and vinegar.

Repeat the layering twice more until all the ingredients are used up.

Dress with any remaining juice from the avocado bowl.

DRESSINGS

The most common types of salad dressing are based on vinaigrette or 'French dressing', which is normally three parts oil to one part vinegar, whisked or blended into an emulsion. They are then flavoured with herbs, salt and honey. Other types of dressings use yoghurt or mayonnaise, which make them creamy.

A good salad dressing is a real digestive aid and the oils make the dry vegetables moist.

Spicy Miso Dressing

1 tsp tahini

2 tbsp tamari

2 tbsp balsamic vinegar

2 tbsp water

2 tsp raw honey

2 tbsp brown rice miso or barley miso

2 tbsp hemp or linseed oil

4 tbsp cold pressed sesame oil

½ tsp Chinese five spice

Blend all the ingredients together in a food processor.

Use it to pour over your favourite salads.

Store in a jar and shake well, or whisk, before using.

Tamarini & Chive Dressing

This dressing benefits from the natural saltiness of the
tamari and the creaminess of the tahini.

6 tbsp extra virgin olive oil

3 tbsp hemp oil or linseed oil

1 lemon *juiced*

2 tbsp tamari

1 tsp tahini

1 tsp raw honey

1 tbsp chopped fresh chives

In a food processor or liquidiser blend together
the oils, lemon juice, tamari, honey and tahini.

Add the fresh herbs.

Store in a jar and pour over your favourite salads.

Shake well or whisk again before using.

Pesto

This dish dates back to ancient Roman times, when they made a similar paste from cheese, garlic and herbs. The name derives from the Latin word 'pisto', which means 'to grind' and is also why a hand grinder is called a 'pestle'. The Italians added basil, but it wasn't until the 1980s that it became popular in the USA before spreading to the UK. Good as a dip or marinade, particularly with pasta dishes. It will store well in the fridge for five days or can be frozen.

100 g fresh basil

125 ml olive or hemp oil

75 g pine nuts

75 g Parmesan cheese *grated*

2 garlic cloves *peeled*

¼ tsp salt

pinch of ground black pepper

1 tbsp lemon juice

Pick over the basil, discarding black leaves, tough stems, etc. Wash in cold water and spin or pat dry.

Blend the basil and oil in a food processor or liquidiser.

Dry roast the pine nuts in a pan until lightly toasted, taking care to keep them moving to prevent them from burning.

Add the nuts and garlic to the oil and basil.

Blend again until smooth.

Add the lemon juice and grated Parmesan cheese.

Season with salt and pepper.

Superfood Sensation

This thick, rich and nutritious preparation can be used both as a dressing on salads and as a dip for cooked vegetables. It also makes a fantastic pâté or sandwich spread if you omit the kefir/yoghurt. The miso and kefir are packed with probiotic bacteria, and work together with the barley grass and nori flakes to make this a superfood sensation!

4 tbsp tahini

2 tbsp miso

1 tsp dried parsley

1½ tsp barley grass powder

1 tsp nori flakes

100 ml kefir or live yoghurt optional

Mix all the ingredients together slowly to prevent the barley grass from flying into the air.

Can be stored in a jar in the fridge.

Keith's Vinaigrette

This simple dressing brings any salad to life. It can be used on hot vegetables or as a marinade and can be stored for several days.

120 ml extra virgin olive oil

4 tbsp apple juice

2 tbsp balsamic vinegar

2-3 garlic cloves *peeled*

1 tbsp Dijon mustard

1 tbsp raw honey

Blend together all of the ingredients in a food processor. If you wish, after blending add some freshly chopped herbs of your choice.

Store in a jar. Shake well or whisk before using.

Pour over your favourite salads.

CONDIMENTS

In Ayurveda, there are six tastes: sweet, salty, bitter, sour, pungent and astringent. A meal should ideally contain all of them to improve digestion and stimulate your whole being.

Western diets are generally too sweet, too salty and sometimes overly pungent (hot, spicy). The other tastes (bitter, sour and astringent) tend to be infrequent or entirely missing from our diet.

To ensure you are getting enough of each taste, use my Ayurvedic 'Six Taste Spice Mix' (pictured left), which has all the tastes included. Sprinkle it like magic powder on your food. It stimulates your six taste buds and activates the Ayurvedic energies in your body.

Six Taste Spice Mix

Fennel and cardamom provide the sweet taste in this mixture; ginger and pepper are the main pungent (hot) flavours. The salt makes it salty and fenugreek gives it the bitter taste. Amchur is dried unripe mango powder, which is very sour. The remaining astringent taste comes from the turmeric.

20 green cardamom pods

1 tsp fennel seeds

1 tsp black peppercorns

1 tsp Himalayan salt

1 tsp ground turmeric

1 tsp ground coriander

1 tsp ground ginger

½ tsp ground fenugreek

½ tsp dried mango powder (amchur)

Open the cardamom pods to release the seeds.

Put the seeds into a grinder or pulverise them using a pestle and mortar.

Add the fennel seeds and peppercorns to the cardamom seeds and grind into a powder.

Add the salt.

Stir in the remaining ground spices.

I recommend using this at the table instead of salt and pepper. If stored in a sealed jar, it will keep for a few weeks.

Vegetable Sides

Vegetables are the most alkalising of foods and full of natural phytonutrients. I generally make 50 per cent of my diet vegetables, either eaten raw in the warmer months (freshly juiced or in salads), or cooked in soups, stews and other savoury dishes during the colder months of the year.

They are particularly tasty when cooked in a way that still lets you appreciate their natural colours and flavours.

Light cooking, such as steaming and stir frying, can help make vegetables more digestible. Serving them straight after cooking retains their natural vitality or prana, so it's important that at least part of your meal is eaten freshly cooked if not raw.

Side dishes are designed to add colour, texture and interest to a meal. You may find that some of these dishes are satisfying enough to take centre stage, particularly if they have good protein content and you spice them up a bit.

Most of these recipes use simple techniques that work with any vegetables that are in season or need using up at the end of the week. The Ayurvedic rule of thumb is to use local and seasonal produce whenever possible.

Samia's Spicy Potato Dish

This recipe is all about the spices, in this case Samia's secret spice blend. It has been handed down in whispers for generations, so don't tell anyone. Or if you do, ask them not to tell anyone else.

Serves 2-3

THE POTATO DISH

500 g white potatoes *peeled & diced*

½ tsp cumin seeds

5 whole peppercorns

5 tsp Samia's secret spice mix

1 large red onion *finely sliced*

2 garlic cloves *crushed*

1½ tbsp ghee

10 g butter

3 tomatoes *peeled & chopped*

½ tsp salt *or to taste*

1½ tbsp lemon juice

1 tbsp chopped fresh coriander

SAMIA'S SECRET-ISH SPICE MIX

Mix together:

1 part Madras curry powder

7 parts ground paprika

5 parts ground coriander

1 part ground turmeric

Steam the potatoes for 20 minutes, or until tender.

Meanwhile melt the ghee in a non-stick pan.

Add the cumin seeds and cook for a few seconds until fragrant.

Add the crushed garlic and cook for half a minute, stirring constantly. Add the 5 teaspoons of Samia's spice mix and the peppercorns. Stir for a few seconds.

Add the onion and the salt, with a little extra butter to maintain a moist consistency.

Cover with a tight lid and cook on a very low heat until the onions are soft. Stir occasionally so it doesn't stick. The steam generated will make the onions really tender. Reduce the heat or add a little water if the mixture begins to stick or burn.

When the onion is nicely caramelised, add the chopped tomatoes. Simmer for about 10 minutes until the tomatoes have become saucy.

Add the lemon juice and fresh coriander.

Carefully mix with the steamed potatoes, folding the ingredients together to avoid mushing them.

Homemade Garam Masala

You can, of course, use a ready-made garam masala, but I find that this homemade version really brings the next three recipes to life. 'Garam' means hot and 'masala' means mix—so it's traditionally a mixture of warming spices. It's also more authentic than curry powder, which was really a relatively recent concoction for European tastes.

Spices such as pepper and clove provide the heat (better to use than chilli powder, which can overpower the other tastes and irritate the digestive system) while other spices such as cinnamon and cardamom add a depth of flavour. All of them assist digestion.

1 tbsp coriander seeds

1½ tsp cumin seed

1 tsp black peppercorns

1 cm cinnamon stick

½ tsp cardamom seeds
(seeds from about 10 pods)

½ tsp fennel seed

6 whole cloves

2 dried bay leaves

Toast all the spices in a small pan until they are aromatic and slightly roasted.

Allow to cool then tip into a spice grinder or use a pestle and mortar.

Grind to a fine powder, and store in an airtight jar.

Fresh is best, so try to use it within a week or two.

Ayurvedic Sweet Potato Curry

This is a classic Indian dish based on Ayurvedic
wisdom and use of spices. To reduce the kapha
qualities of this dish, we use sweet potatoes
instead of regular potatoes.

Serves 2-3

2 tbsp ghee or coconut oil

½ tsp cumin seeds

60 ml fresh cream

generous pinch of asafoetida

1 tsp ground paprika

1 tsp ground coriander

½ tsp ground turmeric

2 medium sweet potatoes *peeled & diced*

250 g frozen peas

350 ml vegetable stock

1 tsp garam masala *homemade is best*

salt & pepper *to taste*

1 tbsp chopped fresh coriander

FOR THE CURRY PASTE

1 medium onion *peeled & chopped*

1 large tomato *chopped*

1 tsp grated fresh ginger

3-4 garlic cloves *peeled & chopped*

To make the curry paste place the onion, tomato, ginger and garlic in a liquidiser or food processor. Blend until smooth. Put this aside for later.

Heat the ghee/coconut oil in a large pan and cook the cumin seeds gently until slightly fragrant.

Add the prepared curry paste, mix well and then stir in the cream. Sauté this until the oil starts to separate from the sides of the pan and the sauce begins to thicken. Then add the asafoetida, ground coriander, paprika and turmeric.

Stir in the sweet potatoes and add the stock.

Reheat, cover and simmer for about 15 minutes or until the vegetables are just tender.

Add the frozen peas and simmer for another few minutes.

Sprinkle in the garam masala and stir well. Season with salt and pepper.

Garnish with the fresh coriander.

Ayurvedic Spicy Thickpeas with Karela

Karela (also called bitter gourd) is a cucumber-like vegetable. As its name suggests it's very bitter, so much so that it's an Ayurvedic medicine in its own right. The strong taste stimulates digestion and bile production in the liver. Cooked properly like this, it makes a delicious side dish. Amchur (dried mango powder) is available in Indian spice shops and has a sour taste—a bit like lemon.

Serves 2-3

1 medium karela

1 tbsp ghee or coconut oil

1 large onion *peeled & thinly sliced*

2 garlic cloves *crushed*

2 tsp grated fresh ginger

2 large tomatoes *peeled & finely chopped*

1 tsp ground turmeric

½ tsp amchur mango powder *optional*

1 tsp garam masala *homemade is best*

1 tsp ground coriander

pinch of chilli powder

salt *to taste*

1 tsp grated jaggery *optional*

400 g tin chickpeas *rinsed & drained*

1 tbsp kefir or live yoghurt

1 tbsp chopped fresh coriander

Cut the karela in half, scoop out and discard the seeds, then slice finely. Steam it until tender, which takes about 10 minutes.

Meanwhile heat the ghee/coconut oil in a pan. Add the onion, ginger and garlic and sauté on low to medium heat until the onion slices become tender.

Add the peeled tomatoes, turmeric, amchur, garam masala, coriander and chilli.

Stir fry until the tomatoes are partially cooked.

Stir in the steamed karela and chick peas.

Add the jaggery. Season with salt to taste.

Cover the pan. Simmer for another 5 minutes.

Garnish with the chopped fresh coriander and kefir/yoghurt.

Spinach Paneer

Paneer is a simple unfermented cheese that keeps its shape when cooked. It's the only cheese recommended in Ayurvedic cooking. Palak (spinach) paneer is my favourite way of eating it. You could buy the garam masala or use my homemade version. This spinach sauce can also be used to coat other cooked vegetables or beans. It can also be diluted with a little vegetable stock to make a spicy soup.

Serves 3-4

2 tbsp ghee or coconut oil

200 g paneer *cut into cubes*

1 onion *peeled & roughly chopped*

2 garlic cloves *peeled*

1 tomato

1 tsp grated fresh ginger

1 tsp garam masala

½ tsp ground turmeric

250 g fresh spinach *chopped*

120 ml cream or coconut milk

½ tsp salt

1 tbsp chopped fresh coriander

Liquidise the onion, garlic, tomato and ginger in a food processor or blender.

Add half the ghee/coconut oil to a frying pan and sauté the paneer gently until golden, then set aside for later. Drain any excess ghee/oil into a larger saucepan and add the other half of the ghee/oil.

Sauté the liquidised onion mixture for about 5 minutes.

Add the ground spices.

Cook for a further few minutes.

Stir in the cream/coconut milk and spinach. Reheat and simmer for 5 minutes. Liquidise to make a thick sauce (a stick blender is good for this).

Add the paneer and reheat.

Garnish with the fresh coriander.

Curried Winter Vegetables

Serves 2-3

1 tbsp ghee or coconut oil

¼ tsp black mustard seeds

1 leek *sliced*

½ tsp ground cumin

¼ tsp ground coriander

¼ tsp ground turmeric

100 g white cabbage *finely sliced*

3 medium carrots *peeled & sliced*

pinch of chilli powder

¼ tsp cinnamon

1½ tbsp lemon juice

salt *to taste*

1 tbsp chopped fresh coriander

In a medium-sized pan heat the ghee/coconut oil and add the mustard seeds. Once sizzling, cover the pan and wait for the mustard seeds to pop. Remove from the heat and wait for them to finish crackling. Then add the leek slices and replace on the heat. Sauté the leeks until they soften, then add the ground cumin, coriander and turmeric and continue sautéing for a few minutes.

Add the carrots and cabbage and reheat, then stir in the cinnamon and chilli powder.

Cover the pan, reduce the heat and let it simmer in its own steam for 5 minutes. Stir and make sure the spices don't stick to the bottom of the pan.

Replace the lid and cook for another 5 minutes. Stir again and repeat the cycle until all the vegetables are tender, which will take about 20 minutes in total. Remove the lid, stir in the lemon juice and season with salt. Garnish with the fresh coriander.

Brussels Sprouts with Lemon & Yoghurt Sauce

Lemon juice transforms Brussels sprouts; so much so that children will actually eat them! In this recipe they are baked and steamed in their own juice.

Serves 2-3

300 g Brussels sprouts

2 tbsp coconut oil

1 tbsp chopped fresh chives

1 tbsp lemon juice

50 g kefir or thick live yoghurt

salt & pepper *to taste*

Preheat the oven to 180 °C.

Place the sprouts in a baking dish, melt the coconut oil in a pan and pour over the vegetables.

Cover tightly with foil and bake until tender, about 30 minutes.

Meanwhile, whisk together the kefir/yoghurt, chives and lemon juice.

Season with salt and pepper.

Remove the vegetables from the oven, take off the foil and pour the sauce over the warm sprouts.

Sesame Ginger Steamed Broccoli

This is a wonderful Macrobiotic recipe that seasons the broccoli without overpowering its natural taste. Mirin is a sweet rice wine that has a low alcohol content but adds a depth of flavour and natural sheen to the dish. If you can't find mirin, use a natural teriyaki sauce, which contains mirin and soya sauce.

Serves 2-3

500 g broccoli *cut into florets*

2 tbsp mirin & 1 tbsp tamari, or 3 tbsp teriyaki sauce

1 tbsp grated fresh ginger

1 tsp sesame oil

100 ml vegetable stock

pinch of salt

1 tsp sesame seeds

Place the broccoli, mirin & tamari/teriyaki, ginger, oil and stock in large pan.

Cover, and bring to a simmer over a medium heat. Steam for 4 minutes, or until the broccoli is bright green and crisp-tender. Add a little more stock if it dries out.

Dry-roast the sesame seeds in a saucepan.

Add the salt and grind with a pestle and mortar.

Sprinkle over the cooked broccoli.

Papas Arrugadas
Wrinkly Potatoes

The modern potato originates in the Canary Isles. Traditionally they were cooked in sea water and lemon, then drained. As they dried out the salt crystalised and they went wrinkly, hence the Spanish name papas arrugadas, meaning wrinkly potatoes. They, of course, needed the perfect sauce, which was called mojo sauce—a delicious hybrid of traditional ingredients and others newly discovered from South America.

Serves 3

1 kg small new potatoes

2 tbsp sea salt

1 litre of water

½ lemon *in chunky slices*

Put all the ingredients into a pan.

Bring to the boil.

Simmer for 20 minutes, or until tender.

Drain most of the water.

Remove the lemon.

Turn off the heat and gently shake the pot so that the salt dries and crystallises on the potatoes.

Mojo Rojo
Red Sauce

The raw pepper and paprika give this a fresh vibrant colour. This is a raw food dressing that adds sparkle to a meal. Traditionally served with wrinkly potatoes (opposite), this could also be used as a sauce on all sorts of fresh vegetable or bean dishes.

Serves 2-3

2 garlic cloves *peeled*

2 tbsp extra virgin olive oil

1 tbsp white wine vinegar

1 tsp ground paprika

1 tsp ground cumin

1 large red pepper
deseeded & roughly chopped

salt *to taste*

Keeping the salt to one side, place all the other ingredients in a liquidiser or food processor and blend until they become a smooth purée.

Season to taste.

Pour over the freshly cooked potatoes.

Mojo Verde
Green Sauce

The sister sauce to the red mojo rojo, this one is bright green, courtesy of the green pepper and fresh coriander. The vibrant colours of both sauces are a feast for the eyes. Both are great served with freshly cooked potatoes.

Serves 2-3

2 garlic cloves *peeled*

2 tbsp extra virgin olive oil

1 tbsp white wine vinegar

1 handful of fresh coriander

½ tsp ground cumin

1 large green pepper *deseeded & chopped*

salt *to taste*

Keeping the salt to one side, place all the other ingredients in a blender or food processor and liquidise until they become a smooth purée. Season to taste.

Herby Carrot & Swede Mash

Serves 2-3

200 g carrots *peeled & diced*

100 g swede *peeled & diced*

1 large garlic clove *crushed*

3 tbsp double cream

1 tbsp finely chopped fresh parsley

1 lemon rind *grated*

salt & pepper *to taste*

1 tsp butter

Preheat the oven to 180°C.

Steam the carrots and swede until tender, about 20 minutes.

Place in a liquidiser or food processor and blend with the garlic and cream until it becomes a creamy purée. Stir in the lemon rind and parsley.

Season to taste with salt and pepper.

Turn into the greased ovenproof dish.

Smooth over with a fork and dot with the butter.

Cook in the oven for about 15–20 minutes.

Samphire with Lemon & Butter

A nutritious and tasty all-in-one! Samphire (sea asparagus) is not just a tasty vegetable, it also gives you a seaweed-like boost of healthy minerals—without having to endure the slimy taste of seaweed. This plant is abundant in estuaries and salt marshes, but be quick because it is only in season from June to August (October to March in the Southern Hemisphere).

Serves 2–3

100 g samphire
remove roots

1 tbsp butter

1 tbsp hemp oil or linseed oil

1 tbsp lemon juice

salt & pepper *to taste*

Wash and rinse the samphire well.

Steam for 5–8 minutes until juicy and tender.

Melt the butter in a pan.

Add the samphire and stir to coat with butter.

Add the lemon juice and hemp/linseed oil.

Season with salt and pepper.

Glazed Carrots with Garlic

This is a bit like honey-glazed carrots. However, as Ayurveda doesn't recommend cooking with honey, I've used jaggery or coconut sugar instead. Alternatively you could use maple or date syrup and the more familiar fennel and cinnamon. This dressing adds an instant oriental magic to any dish.

Serves 2-3

750 g baby carrots

2 garlic cloves *peeled*

500 ml vegetable stock

1 tbsp ghee or coconut oil

1 tsp ground paprika

50 g grated jaggery or coconut sugar

2 tbsp fresh rosemary

Place the carrots and garlic in a large pan and cover with the stock. Bring to the boil, then reduce heat, cover and simmer for about 10 minutes until the vegetables are tender. Drain the carrots and garlic and keep some of the stock.

Place the ghee/coconut oil, jaggery/coconut sugar, paprika, rosemary and 2 tablespoons of the reserved stock in a pan.

Heat until bubbling, then add the carrots and garlic.

Stir and cook for about 5 minutes until the water evaporates and the carrots become slightly caramelised.

Lightly Spiced Seasonal Vegetables

You can use any seasonal vegetables in this dish.
Simply add them in the appropriate order, starting with the
ones that need the longest cooking. When cooked, everything
should be just softened all the way through.

Serves 2-3

100 g fresh peas

100 g French beans *topped & tailed*

2 tbsp ghee or coconut oil

½ tsp cumin seeds

1 medium onion *finely chopped*

2 garlic cloves *crushed*

1 or 2 leeks *sliced*

¼ tsp ground turmeric

pinch of chilli powder

½ tsp ground coriander

pinch of salt

100 g mangetout peas

100 g sugar snap peas

1½ tbsp lemon juice

Steam the fresh peas and French beans for 5–10 minutes until sweet and tender.

Meanwhile put the ghee/coconut oil in a pan over a medium heat and gently fry the cumin seeds.

When they smell fragrant, carefully add the onion.

Fry the onion for about 5 minutes until soft, then add the garlic and leeks.

Cook for a further 5 minutes.

Add the turmeric, chilli powder, coriander and salt, and stir to mix.

Stir in the mangetout and sugar snap peas.

Cook for a further 2 minutes. Stir in the lemon juice, and mix in the peas and beans. Serve immediately.

Spicy Pan Potatoes

These potatoes are made in a saucepan,
but come out looking like they've been roasted!

Serves 2-3

1 tbsp ghee or coconut oil

3 garlic cloves *peeled*

1 tsp ground paprika

½ tsp ground coriander

¼ tsp ground turmeric

1 tsp finely chopped fresh rosemary
or ½ tsp dried rosemary

600 g baby potatoes

300 ml light vegetable stock

2 tbsp chopped fresh coriander

Heat the ghee/coconut oil in a large pan with a tight fitting lid.

Add the paprika, coriander, turmeric and rosemary and then the potatoes.

Sauté the potatoes for 2–3 minutes to make sure they are coated with the oil and spices.

Add the stock and the garlic cloves and bring to the boil. Cover the pan and simmer for 20 minutes, or until tender. Stir occasionally so that the potatoes cook evenly.

Remove the lid and cook gently to boil off the remaining stock, stirring occasionally so that the potatoes don't stick.

Garnish with fresh coriander.

Curried Spring Vegetables

Vary the vegetables according to season and what you have in the fridge.
You could use carrots, swedes or butternut squash instead of the sweet
potato, and leeks or sliced courgettes instead of the asparagus.

Serves 2-3

2 tbsp ghee or coconut oil

1 tsp black mustard seeds

1 tsp ginger *grated*

1 red onion *sliced*

2 garlic cloves *crushed*

pinch of chilli powder

½ tsp ground turmeric

1 tsp ground coriander

1 sweet potato *peeled & diced*

250 ml coconut milk

250 g asparagus tips or
sliced green beans

1 red pepper *deseeded & diced*

¼ tsp salt

1 tbsp chopped fresh coriander

In a large pan, melt the ghee/coconut oil over medium
heat. Carefully add the mustard seeds. Once sizzling,
cover the pan and wait for the mustard seeds to pop.
Remove from the heat and wait for them to finish
crackling.

Carefully add the onion, ginger and garlic. Return to the
heat and cook for another two or three minutes. Now stir
in the chilli, turmeric and coriander. Then add the sweet
potato and coconut milk. Bring to the boil, then reduce
the heat and simmer. Cook for a further 10 minutes or so,
stirring occasionally.

Now add the asparagus tips/green beans and pepper
to the sweet potato mix. Cover and simmer for another
10–15 minutes, or until the vegetables are tender. Add a
little vegetable stock if the mixture begins to dry out.

Mix in the salt and garnish with fresh coriander.

Vegetable Pakoras

Pakoras are made using gram flour, which is made from chickpeas. It's used a lot in Indian cooking because it makes a superb eggless batter. This is popularly mixed with spices and vegetables and then fried. We may not consider deep frying as a healthy preparation method, but in this case the vegetables are lightly cooked and the gram flour is high in protein.

Serves 4

1 onion *finely chopped*

1 small carrot *diced small*

1 small courgette *diced small*

200 g gram flour

¼ tsp bicarbonate of soda

200 ml cold water *approx*

½ tsp salt

pinch of asafoetida

1 tsp garam masala

¼ tsp onion seeds (nigella seeds)

pinch of chilli powder

1 tsp ground coriander

½ tsp ground turmeric

handful of fresh coriander *chopped*

500 ml ghee for deep frying

Chop all the vegetables quite finely as they have to cook in the batter. Sieve the gram flour to remove lumps. Mix in enough water to make a thick batter, and whisk. Stir in the baking soda, salt and all the spices and mix well. Then add the fresh coriander and prepared vegetables. It should be the consistency of pancake batter; add more flour if it's too runny, or water if it's too thick.

Heat the ghee in a pan on medium heat for deep frying. Test the temperature by adding a teaspoon of batter. It will float once the ghee is hot enough. Using two tablespoons drop small balls of the battered vegetables into the hot fat. Do not touch them for a few seconds or they will break up.

After a little time move them around and fry till they become golden brown on all sides. They need to fry for 3–4 minutes to make sure the vegetables are cooked. Reduce the heat if they brown too quickly, or increase slightly if they are taking too long. When cooked, remove them with a metal sieve and place them on kitchen paper to absorb any excess ghee.

Main
Dishes

The purpose of a main course is to be the highlight of any meal—just like my wife was at our wedding. Her eight bridesmaids were like the side dishes, they complemented the bride but in no way outshone her.

*I*n French dining the main course follows an entrée or starter. In the USA and parts of Canada, however, the entrée is the main course, so it can get a bit confusing. Hors d'oeuvre is another name for a starter, meaning literally 'apart from the main'.

Here at the Dru Centre we've unintentionally mimicked French dining and combined it with Ayurvedic principles.

I call it 'A-la-vedic'.

Our entrée is usually a seasonal vegetable soup, fortified with lentils or barley. This is followed by the main course: a substantial high protein vegetarian dish which includes pulses, with nuts and seeds for extra protein. This is served with vegetables and a carbohydrate such as potatoes or rice.

We are one of the few British institutions that have truly embraced our European cousin's dining habits by taking at least one hour over lunch and not feeling guilty about it. I think it has even become part of our yoga philosophy!

We also encourage the enjoyment of good company, eating slowly and really savouring the tastes.

The only thing missing is good wine. My answer to that is fresh vegetable juice. It even looks like wine if you include beetroot! It livens me up, not with inebriation, but with its natural, living, vibrant energy. It really helps to top up my feel-good hormones much better than alcohol!

KEITH-CHERI

The easiest way to make a main dish which contains enough protein is to simply mix pulses and grains together. In India this type of dish is called kitcheri and it is one of the staple foods in northern parts of India.

Kitcheri is a generic term for rice and pulses cooked together—cleverly making them more nutritious and easy-to-digest while providing a complete protein dish. In Ayurvedic medicine, kitcheri is used as a convalescent food.

Here are some of my great Keith-cheri recipes, so-called because they are my own variations of these classic dishes.

Kitcheri should
be moist but
not soupy

Mung Bean & Brown Rice Keith-cheri

This recipe involves soaking whole mung beans overnight to start them germinating—thus allowing them to cook more quickly and making them easier to digest. Both mung beans and short grain brown rice are soothing to the digestive system when well cooked, making this the most nurturing of recipes.

Serves 2-3

100 g short grain brown rice

100 g whole mung beans *soaked overnight*

100 ml vegetable stock or water

1 carrot *diced*

1 small potato *peeled & diced*

1 celery stick *sliced*

1 small leek *sliced*

1 tbsp ghee

1 red onion *finely chopped*

½ tsp whole cumin seeds

½ tsp mustard seeds

2 tsp ginger root *grated*

½ tsp ground coriander

½ tsp ground cumin

½ tsp ground turmeric

pinch of asafoetida

3 tbsp lemon juice

1 tsp grated jaggery *optional*

salt & pepper *to taste*

handful fresh coriander *chopped*

Drain the pre-soaked beans and place in a large pan with a good lid. Add the stock/water and rice, cover and simmer for 20 minutes.

Now add the vegetables, except for the onion. Reheat and cover.

Simmer for another 20 minutes or until the beans, rice and vegetables are soft. Add more stock/water if it starts to dry out at any point. The consistency should be moist but not sloppy.

In a separate saucepan, sauté the cumin and mustard seeds in the ghee. Once sizzling, cover the pan and wait for the mustard seeds to pop.

Remove from the heat and wait for them to finish crackling.

Carefully add the onion, ginger and all the powdered spices. Reheat and simmer for several minutes until the onion and spices are cooked.

Allow it to cool. Stir the sautéed onion/spice mix into the cooked beans and rice.

Reheat and season to taste. Add the lemon juice and jaggery.

Garnish with the fresh coriander.

Spicy Quinoa Keith-cheri with Lentils

Here, for a modern twist, I've used quinoa instead of rice.

Serves 4

100 g red lentils *washed*

2 tbsp ghee or coconut oil

1 small sweet potato *peeled & diced*

1 medium onion *sliced*

1 carrot *sliced*

2 garlic cloves *crushed*

½ tsp mild curry powder

¼ tsp ground cumin

¼ tsp ground turmeric

pinch of ground ginger

pinch of ground allspice

750 ml vegetable stock

150 g quinoa *rinsed*

½ tsp salt

1 tsp ground black pepper

Heat the ghee/coconut oil in a large pot over medium heat. Add the sweet potato, onion, carrot and garlic and stir well. Cook for about 5 minutes, or until the vegetables are tender.

Stir in the powdered spices.

Sauté for a further 5 minutes.

Add the lentils and pour in the stock.

Reheat and bring to the boil.

Cover and cook for 10 minutes, stirring occasionally.

Add the quinoa. Cover and cook for another 10 minutes, stirring occasionally.

Add more stock if it dries out too much before the lentils or quinoa are cooked.

Season to taste with salt and pepper.

Luxury Keith-cheri

I have added seaweed in this recipe for additional minerals.
Also its delicious sliminess actually lubricates the food and soothes digestion.

Serves 4

100 g split mung beans

100 g basmati rice

1 tbsp ghee or coconut oil

½ tsp black mustard seeds

½ tsp fennel seeds

¼ tsp ground cinnamon

½ tsp ground turmeric

½ tsp ground cumin

½ tsp ground coriander

2 tsp grated fresh ginger

75 g sweet potato *peeled & diced*

75 g carrots *peeled & diced*

75 g courgettes *diced*

750 ml vegetable stock

1 stick of kombu seaweed

salt & pepper *to taste*

Rinse the mung beans and rice in several changes of water then drain.

In a large pan, melt the ghee/coconut oil. Add the mustard and fennel seeds. Once sizzling, cover the pan and wait for the mustard seeds to pop. Remove from the heat and wait for them to finish crackling.

Carefully add the cinnamon, turmeric, cumin, coriander and ginger; reheat and cook for a few seconds.

Remove from the heat and allow to cool.

Then add the beans, rice and prepared vegetables to the spice mix. Cover with the stock, and add the kombu stick.

Bring to the boil, lower heat, cover and simmer for about 30-35 minutes.

Add a little more stock or water if it dries out.

Season with salt and pepper.

Green Dragon Stew

Serves 4

150 g whole mung beans

750 ml vegetable stock

1 bay leaf

½ tsp ground turmeric

1 tbsp ghee or coconut oil

1 onion *chopped*

1 tomato *sliced*

1 tsp grated fresh ginger

3 garlic cloves *peeled & chopped*

2 tsp garam masala

1 tsp grated jaggery
or coconut sugar *optional*

salt & pepper *to taste*

2 tbsp fresh coriander *chopped*

Cover the beans with the stock, add the bay leaf and turmeric. Bring to the boil, cover and simmer until the beans are tender (30–40 minutes). Add more water if necessary to cover the beans; it needs to remain sloppy.

Meanwhile, place the onion, ginger, tomato and garlic into a liquidiser and liquidise almost to a paste.

Heat the ghee/coconut oil in a pan, add the paste and sauté for about 10 minutes. Stir occasionally so it does not stick.

Add the garam masala and cook for a few minutes.

Mix the tomato mixture with the mung beans when they are cooked. Reheat and let it simmer for a few minutes.

Stir in the jaggery/coconut sugar and season to taste with salt and pepper.

Garnish with the fresh coriander and serve.

Split Peas with Courgettes

Serves 3

100 g yellow split peas

400 ml vegetable stock

2 tbsp ghee or coconut oil

½ tsp mustard seeds

pinch of asafoetida

½ tsp ground turmeric

1 red onion

2 garlic cloves *crushed*

1 tsp ground coriander

1 tsp curry powder

2 medium courgettes *diced*

2 tomatoes *peeled & chopped*

100g spinach *washed & dried*

1 tsp jaggery *optional*

½ tsp salt

1 tbsp chopped fresh coriander

Rinse the split peas a few times until the water runs clear, then drain. Place them with the stock in a saucepan and bring to the boil. Skim off any foam.

Reduce the heat and simmer for 45–60 minutes, until the peas are soft and tender. Add more stock if the peas start to dry out.

Meanwhile, heat the ghee/coconut oil in a dry pan with a lid, and add the mustard seeds. Once sizzling, cover the pan and wait for the mustard seeds to pop. Remove from the heat and wait for them to finish popping. Carefully add the powdered spices, garlic, onion and courgettes. Stir and cook over a medium heat for 5 minutes. Add the tomatoes and spinach. Cook for a few more minutes.

Combine with the cooked split peas. Reheat and simmer for about 10 minutes over a low heat. Stir occasionally to prevent sticking.

Add the jaggery and season to taste with salt.

Garnish with the fresh coriander.

Vegetable & Bean Crumble

This vegetarian main course makes a satisfying dish for everyone to enjoy. We often use gluten-free bread for the breadcrumbs to cater for visitors on wheat-free diets.

Serves 4

350 g butternut squash *peeled & diced*

2 tbsp ghee or coconut oil

1 onion *chopped*

2 garlic cloves *finely chopped*

350 g tomatoes *peeled & chopped*

1 bay leaf

½ tsp thyme *fresh or dried*

½ tsp basil *fresh or dried*

500 ml vegetable stock

¼ tsp black pepper

salt *to taste*

1 tin butter beans *rinsed & drained*

FOR THE CRUMBLE TOPPING

200 g breadcrumbs

100 g walnuts *finely chopped*

2 tbsp fresh rosemary *chopped*

4 tbsp fresh parsley *chopped*

50 g butter

Preheat the oven to 180°C.

With about half of the ghee/coconut oil, roast the butternut squash in a deep baking tray for about 30 minutes or until just tender.

Meanwhile heat the rest of the ghee/coconut oil in a large pan, add the onion and fry for 5 minutes, or until lightly browned. Add the garlic, tomatoes, bay leaf, thyme, basil, stock and pepper, and bring to the boil.

Reduce the heat and simmer for 20 mins.

Season to taste.

Stir the butter beans into the sauce.

Pour the sauce over the roasted squash in the baking tray.

For the topping

Mix together the breadcrumbs, walnuts and herbs then rub in the butter.

Sprinkle the topping over the squash dish in the baking tray.

Return to the oven and bake for 25 minutes until the crumble is golden and crisp.

Black Urid & Sweet Potato Dhal

Dhal is the Indian name for split pulses like red lentils. It is also the generic name for thick stews made with these pulses. This recipe uses split urid beans. These black beans are prized in Ayurveda as a nourishing winter food because they are particularly high in protein and other nutrients.

Serves 4

2 tbsp ghee or coconut oil

1 onion *sliced*

2 carrots *peeled & diced*

250 g sweet potatoes *peeled & diced*

2 garlic cloves *crushed*

2 curry or bay leaves

1 tbsp curry powder

250 g tomatoes *peeled & chopped*

200 g split black urid beans *rinsed well*

600 ml vegetable stock

handful fresh coriander *chopped*

1½ tbsp lemon juice

salt & pepper *to taste*

Warm the ghee/coconut oil in a large saucepan. Add the onion, carrots and sweet potatoes. Cook the vegetables for about 8 minutes or until slightly softened. Stir occasionally.

Add the garlic, curry/bay leaves and curry powder and cook, stirring for 1 minute or until fragrant. Then stir in the tomatoes, urid beans and stock.

Bring to the boil, cover, reduce the heat and simmer gently for 35 minutes or until the beans are tender. If the mixture gets too dry, add a little more stock.

Finally, add the fresh coriander and lemon juice. Season to taste with salt and pepper.

Pumpkin Bake with Courgette

A fresh pumpkin speaks to us of autumn, as do golden leaves falling from the trees. This is a warming and nutritious dish. The saltiness of the stock and tamari, the sourness of the lemon and the warmth of the black pepper help reduce the vata dosha in the changeable autumnal season.

Serves 3-4

100 g red lentils

2 tbsp coconut oil

1 red onion finely *sliced*

2 garlic cloves *crushed*

1 bay leaf

1 tbsp chopped fresh sage

¼ tsp black pepper

500 g pumpkin or squash *peeled & diced*

200 g courgette *sliced*

1 tbsp tamari

250 ml vegetable stock

1 ½ tbsp lemon juice

Preheat the oven to 180 °C.

Heat the oil in a pan, add the onion and garlic, and cook for 2–3 minutes. Stir in the bay leaf, sage and pepper and sauté for 3 minutes.

Add the pumpkin/squash and courgette, cook until slightly softened, then add the lentils, tamari and stock.

Cover the pan, and cook gently for 20 minutes until the vegetables are just tender. Stir occasionally so they don't stick. Add the lemon juice and season to taste.

Transfer to a baking tray.

Bake for 25 minutes.

Green Lentil Shepherd's Pie

Green lentils provide a wholesome base for
this traditional dish. You could also use sweet
potatoes for the mash which gives you a
wonderful orange-coloured topping.

Serves 4

25 g butter or coconut oil

1 onion *chopped*

1 carrot *diced*

75 g swede *peeled & diced*

2 garlic cloves *peeled & finely chopped*

80 g mushrooms *sliced*

1 bay leaf

1 tsp dried thyme

200 g green lentils

750 ml vegetable stock

1 tsp yeast extract

1 tsp tamari

2 tbsp tomato purée

salt & pepper *to taste*

FOR THE MASH

1 kg potatoes *peeled & diced*

85 g butter

100 ml milk

salt & pepper *to taste*

You will need a baking dish that is about 20 cm square.

In a large pan, sauté the onion, swede, carrots and garlic for 5 minutes in the butter/coconut oil.

Add the mushrooms, herbs, lentils and vegetable stock.

Reheat, cover and simmer for 40 minutes. Add a bit more stock if it starts to dry out; don't make it too runny or the potato will sink to the bottom when you come to make the pie.

At this point, switch the oven on to 180°C and make the mashed potato.

For the mashed potato

Cover the potatoes in water and cook until tender, about 15–20 minutes. Drain well and mash the potatoes with the butter and milk. Season to taste with salt and pepper.

When the lentils are soft, stir in the tomato purée, yeast extract and tamari. Season to taste with salt and pepper.

Place the lentil mix into a baking dish.

Top with the mash and smooth over with a fork.

Bake for about 30 minutes.

Moussaka

This is like the lasagne of the east—another layered dish with a cheesy sauce, this time using potatoes and aubergine instead of pasta. Like a lot of rustic cuisine, the exact ingredients can vary. In Greece and the Middle East it is made with aubergines; in eastern Europe more potatoes are used. I use passata which is a light tomato sauce. If you don't have this, peel another 250 grams of fresh tomatoes and liquidise in a blender or food processor.

Serves 4

500 g potatoes *peeled & cut into thick slices*

1 aubergine *sliced*

1 onion *chopped*

2 garlic cloves *crushed*

2 red peppers *cut into large dice*

2 tbsp chopped fresh thyme, or 1 tsp dried thyme

4 tbsp extra virgin olive oil

250g tomatoes *peeled & chopped*

250 ml passata

1 tin chickpeas *rinsed & drained*

300 ml natural live yogurt or kefir

3 eggs

25 g Parmesan cheese *grated*

Preheat the oven to 180°C.

Parboil the potatoes for 5 minutes in salted water or stock. Drain and place in a deep baking tray with the aubergine, onion, garlic and peppers.

Sprinkle with the thyme and drizzle with the olive oil. Roast in the oven for 20 minutes. Carefully turn the vegetables two or three times so they cook evenly.

Add the chopped tomatoes and bake for another 5 minutes.

Remove from the oven, add the chickpeas and spoon the passata over the vegetables.

Beat the eggs and yoghurt together, then stir in the Parmesan cheese. Pour this over the vegetable dish.

Return to the oven and bake for 25 minutes, or until the topping is firm and slightly golden.

Bolognese Vegetariano

This classic recipe originated in the Bologna area of Italy.
I cook a vegetarian version of the traditional Italian ragu. The
combination of lentils and pasta creates a complete protein.

You could use many types of pasta; we like penne, which is
derived from the Latin word penna for 'feather' or 'quill', also
related to the English word 'pen'. We often use gluten-free
pasta so everyone can enjoy the dish. It also makes a great
filling for Lasagne (page 331).

Serves 4

250 g penne pasta

50 g Parmesan cheese *grated*

FOR THE SAUCE

2 tbsp extra virgin olive oil

1 onion *finely chopped*

2 carrots *finely chopped*

2 celery sticks *finely chopped*

2 garlic cloves *crushed*

1 red pepper *deseeded & diced*

1 courgette *diced*

1 tsp dried mixed herbs

½ tsp ground paprika

2 bay leaves

250 g tomatoes *peeled & chopped*

2 tbsp tomato purée

salt & pepper *to taste*

100 g split red lentils

500 ml vegetable stock

Sauté the onions for about 5 minutes in the olive oil.

Add the carrot, celery and garlic. Cook and stir for about another 4 minutes or until the vegetables begin to soften.

Add the red pepper, courgette, mixed herbs, bay leaves and paprika. Stir and cook for a few minutes more.

Rinse the lentils well in several changes of water, then add to the vegetables. Stir in the chopped tomatoes and tomato purée, and add the vegetable stock.

Bring to the boil, cover and simmer for 30 minutes.

Season to taste with salt and pepper.

Meanwhile, cook the pasta in a large saucepan of salted boiling water, until 'al dente' (meaning cooked until it has started to soften, but the centre remains slightly resistant to being chewed).

Drain the pasta well and top with the tomato and lentil sauce. Sprinkle with the Parmesan cheese.

Lasagne

The filling for this is from the previous Bolognese Vegetariano recipe but using half the quantity. You can, of course, make the full amount and freeze half. Here we are using a different type of pasta: lasagne. Make sure the vegetables are chopped finely so you have nice thin layers in the lasagne. Some lasagne sheets require pre-cooking. Even if it says no pre-cook is required, I still blanch them in boiling salty water for a minute or so for a better result. Just be careful the sheets don't get stuck together in the process.

Serves 4

175 g lasagne *about 10 sheets*

½ quantity of bolognese vegetariano

100g Brie cheese *thinly sliced*

100g baby spinach

CREAMY SAUCE

500 ml milk

50 g butter

3 tbsp wholemeal flour

½ tsp salt

¼ tsp black pepper

200 g mature Cheddar *grated*

Preheat the oven to 180°C.

To make the creamy sauce, melt the butter in a saucepan and stir in the flour. Keep stirring as you cook the flour for a few minutes. Remove from the heat and add the milk a little at a time, stirring constantly, to avoid lumps.

Reheat, still whisking the mixture constantly so that it doesn't stick. Let it simmer for one minute. Remove from the heat.

Stir in the seasonings and half the cheese.

Now place half of the bolognaise sauce in the baking dish and cover with a layer of lasagne sheets. Spread the spinach leaves and Brie slices evenly on top.

Cover with a second layer of lasagne sheets. Place the remaining bolognaise on this and top with the final layer of lasagne. Pour the creamy sauce on top and sprinkle with the rest of the grated cheese. Bake until golden, about 35 minutes.

Mixed Bean Chilli

This is similar to a bolognaise sauce, but with a spicy twist of paprika, chilli and coriander. Great served with rice, or as a potato or pie filling.

Serves 3-4

1 tbsp coconut oil or ghee

1 onion *finely sliced*

2 sticks celery *finely sliced*

1 small red pepper *diced*

1 tsp ground coriander

1 tsp ground cumin

1 courgette *diced*

1 carrot *diced*

2 garlic cloves *crushed*

½ small red chilli *finely chopped*

½ tsp dried oregano

½ tsp mixed herbs

1 tsp ground paprika

300 ml vegetable stock

1 tsp jaggery *optional*

250 g tomatoes *peeled & chopped*

3 tbsp tomato purée

400 g tin kidney beans *rinsed & drained*

salt & pepper *to taste*

Sauté the onion and celery in the ghee/coconut oil for a few minutes. Stir in the red pepper.

Add the ground coriander and cumin and cook for a few more minutes.

Add the courgette and carrot and continue cooking for a few minutes.

Add the garlic, chilli, herbs and paprika. Continue cooking for a few minutes to soften the vegetables.

Stir in the jaggery, chopped tomatoes and tomato purée, then add the stock.

Cover and simmer for 30 minutes, adding a little more stock if it becomes too thick.

When cooked, add the kidney beans to the tomato mixture.

Reheat and season to taste with salt and pepper.

Baked Sweet Potato with Tomato Filling

Many Ayurvedic doctors recommend cutting back on potatoes as they can increase kapha too much. Sweet potatoes make a nice alternative to the jacket spud. This high-protein filling has spices and the pro-biotic kefir to help with digestion.

Serves 5

5 medium-sized sweet potatoes

2 tbsp ghee or coconut oil, *plus extra for greasing the potatoes*

1 onion *finely chopped*

1 carrot *thinly sliced*

½ tsp ground paprika

1 tsp ground cumin

1 red pepper *deseeded & diced*

1 cm ginger *peeled & grated*

2 garlic cloves *finely chopped*

250 g tomatoes *peeled & chopped*

250 ml vegetable stock

5 tbsp tomato purée

50 g lentils *rinsed well & drained*

salt & pepper *to taste*

4 tbsp kefir or thick live yogurt

small bunch parsley *chopped*

Preheat the oven to 180°C.

Grease the sweet potatoes with a little ghee or oil, prick with a sharp knife and place in a tray. Bake for 35–45 minutes, or until tender.

Meanwhile put the ghee in a large pan over a low heat. Add the onion and carrot and cook for 8–10 minutes, stirring regularly until soft.

Stir in the paprika and cumin powder; cook for 1 minute. Stir in the red pepper, ginger and garlic and cook for another minute or so.

Add the tomatoes, stock, washed lentils and tomato purée. Bring to the boil, and simmer for about 40 minutes until everything is cooked and it is thick and sauce-like. Season to taste.

When the sweet potatoes are cooked, remove from the oven and split them in half lengthwise. Fill them generously with the sauce and top each one with a dollop of kefir/yoghurt.

Sprinkle with a little parsley.

Stir Fried Vegetables with Tofu

You can buy marinated tofu or make your own using the recipe overleaf. You can actually use all sorts of vegetables in a stir fry. In fact, it is a good way to use up small amounts of raw vegetables left in the fridge at the end of a week. Cut them all into thin sticks and add them to the pan according to the time they need to cook.

Serves 4

2 tbsp coconut oil

1 onion *sliced*

1 garlic clove *peeled & sliced*

1 carrot *cut into sticks*

2 sticks celery *cut into strips*

1 red pepper *cut into sticks*

75 g mushrooms *sliced*

100 g mangetout

100 g beansprouts

250 g marinated tofu *diced*

Fry the onion and garlic in the coconut oil for a few minutes.

Add the celery and carrot and stir fry over a high heat for about five minutes. Then add the red pepper and stir fry for a few more minutes.

Follow with the mushrooms and mangetout and cook for just a minute or two.

Finally add the beansprouts and stir briefly.

Top with the marinated tofu.

Marinated Tofu

This will make any stir fry come to life. Shitake mushrooms add
a distinctive smoky taste and are thought to be very therapeutic
in Macrobiotic philosophy.

Serves 4

25 g dried shitake mushrooms

100 ml stock

½ tsp dried oregano

1 garlic clove *crushed*

1 tsp arame seaweed

1 tbsp cold-pressed sesame oil

1 tbsp red wine vinegar

1 tbsp tamari

pinch of Chinese 5 spice

250 g tofu *diced*

Start by simmering the mushrooms in the stock for 5 minutes.

Add the oregano, arame and garlic; simmer for a few minutes more.

Add the oil, vinegar, tamari, 5 Chinese spice and tofu.

Allow to simmer until the excess liquid has evaporated. Let the tofu fry in the residual oil for a minute or two, carefully turning it as it cooks.

Stir Fry Sauce

The perfect sauce for the marinated tofu stir fry.

Serves 4

200 ml orange juice

1 tsp cornflour

25 ml toasted sesame oil

1½ tbsp ginger *grated*

3 garlic cloves *crushed*

4 tbsp tamari

3 tbsp honey

Dissolve the cornflour into the orange juice.

Cook the garlic and ginger in the sesame oil for a couple of minutes. Remove from the heat.

Stir in the orange juice /cornflour mix.

Add tthe honey and tamari.

Add this sauce to a stir fry towards the end of the cooking.

It will thicken quickly and glaze the vegetables.

Festive Cashew & Paneer Loaf

This delicious recipe gives you a deluxe version of a nut roast. The cooked brown rice adds body to the dish and, as a special treat, the paneer adds a chewy meatiness. You could actually use any type of cooked rice or quinoa in this dish. For best results use a loaf tin.

Serves 4

100 g cooked brown rice *about 40g when raw*

1 red onion *finely chopped*

1 tbsp coconut oil

100 g paneer *cut into small dice*

50 g sunflower seeds

50 g wholemeal breadcrumbs

100 g cashews

50 g ground almonds

2 tbsp fresh parsley *chopped*

75 ml hot vegetable stock

salt & pepper *to taste*

2 large eggs *beaten*

Preheat the oven to 175°C.

Grease a 450 g loaf tin. You could also line it with baking paper so the nut roast comes out in one piece.

In a large frying pan, gently sauté the onion and paneer in the oil until they are slightly golden.

Finely grind the cashew nuts and sunflower seeds in a processor.

In a separate bowl, mix together the onion and paneer, sunflower seeds, cashews, ground almonds, breadcrumbs and parsley.

Stir in the hot stock and season to taste.

Stir the beaten eggs and cooked rice into the nut mixture until well combined. Press the mixture into the prepared loaf tin.

Bake for 40 minutes or until firm.

Keith's Nut Roast

Serves 4-6

1 onion *sliced*

25 g butter

1 stick celery *sliced*

1 small carrot *grated*

200 g cashews

100 g wholemeal breadcrumbs

1 tsp mixed herbs

240 ml stock

2 tsp yeast extract

1 egg

salt & pepper *to taste*

Preheat the oven to 180°C.

Sauté the onion and celery in the butter until softened.

Add the grated carrot and cook for another 2 minutes. Set aside.

Grind the cashew nuts and mix with the breadcrumbs and the mixed herbs. Stir in the cooked vegetables.

In a small saucepan, bring the stock to the boil. Remove from the heat and stir in the yeast extract.

Add enough stock to the nuts and breadcrumbs to make a moist, but not sloppy, mix.

Set aside to cool for 5-10 minutes.

In a small bowl beat the egg. Add to the nut mixture and stir well.

Turn into a greased loaf tin and bake for 35 minutes, or until the roast feels solid and the top is browned.

Cheeses
& Fruits

A nice piece of cheese can be a great way to finish off your meal. However, the cheese can only be as good as the milk it is made from. Try to get cheeses from the milk of grass-fed animals if you can; they will have a lot more omega-3 fatty acids and other nutrients.

Cheeses made from raw milk can also have extra natural enzymes and beneficial bacteria that aid digestion. In the past there was a risk of harmful pathogens getting into dairy produce unless it was pasteurised. Luckily in the UK raw cheeses are subject to strict safety testing. So now we can have our cheesecake and eat it.

If you can't get raw milk products near where you live there are other great organic cheeses you can try. One of my favourites is Reblochon from the French Alps, where the cows graze on Alpine meadows full of herbs and wildflowers. It's also called the devotional cheese, 'le fromage de dévotion', as it was given to monks in the 16th century by the populace in return for their blessing.

These cheeses are so good that even the smell of them takes you on a journey. I love to open the packet and let the aroma transport me to Alpine pastures, the cows in their shelters and the cool cellars where the cheese matures.

More locally we enjoy Welsh cheeses too, including a Caerphilly cheese that is matured slowly. It's a bit crumbly so you have to open it carefully.

These specialist cheeses are not cheap, costing up to twice as much as a normal Cheddar or up to four times as much as an industrial cheese. But remember that with good cheese less is more. A small piece eaten with awareness is so satisfying that you won't need so much.

That is the French secret to eating: fully appreciate good quality food taken in moderation.

FRUITS

In the UK our green and pleasant land is one of the best places to grow apples. We used to have thousands of different varieties, but a few modern hybrids like Gala and Jazz have taken over. These look good and they store and travel well. But to me they lack the flavour of some of the original varieties.

My favourite heritage apple is the Egremont Russet. It is at its best from October to Christmas time. A recent study found that this type of traditional apple has many times more vitamins and bioflavonoids than a lot of the hybrid varieties. So an apple a day keeps the doctor away—if it's a Russet.

Ayurveda recommends eating seasonal produce. Nature, in a way, can be thought of as a doctor—providing you with the right medicine at the right time.

Strawberries in summer have a cooling effect which stimulates the nervous system and helps counteract summer fatigue. In late summer the blackberries and elderberries are packed with vitamin C and immune-boosting compounds to fortify us for winter. Later in the year we have the more substantial apples and pears, containing antioxidants and digestive enzymes to keep us healthy in the winter months.

Ayurveda also recommends eating raw fruit as a fresh snack between meals as fruit doesn't combine so well with other foods in a main meal.

What could be better as a mid-afternoon snack than a fresh fruit salad served with cream, yoghurt, kefir, or fromage frais with lashings of raw honey? Nature's storehouse provides us with many other great treats, such as fresh nuts, seeds and dried fruit.

Desserts

Again we look across the English Channel for inspiration, this time to Provence in southeast France, where there is a wonderful tradition of the 13 desserts. These are made at Christmas and represent Jesus and his 12 disciples. Many of the dishes have a special meaning. The first four desserts (raisins, almonds, hazelnuts and figs) are called the 'mendicants', literally meaning 'beggars', symbolising the religious orders where members take a vow of poverty. Foremost are the Franciscan monks who follow the example of Saint Francis, founder of one of the first mendicant traditions.

In this dessert symbolism, the Franciscan monks are represented by figs. Then there are raisins for the Dominicans, hazelnuts for the Augustins, and almonds for Carmelite monks and nuns, chosen because these fruits resemble the colour and appearance of the different orders' robes. They are all included in the Mendicant Cookie recipe, where the four traditions are united in a chocolate base.

The fifth dessert dish is simply dates, as they originate in the Holy Land and are a fruit that Jesus and the disciples would have enjoyed. The sixth and seventh desserts were made from nougat. Traditionally, white nougat represented good and black nougat bad, to remind us that in every moment we have a choice of paths to follow. This is served with the eighth dessert of olive oil bread, which is sweetened and flavoured with orange. Olive oil bread is always broken by hand, never cut with a knife. Breaking of the bread with a prayer of thanks is a Jewish custom that predates Christianity.

The other desserts can vary locally or in families. The thirteen desserts are made on Christmas Eve after the great supper. A spare place is laid for a stranger, who may be an angel or ancestor to be welcomed and who can help eat all the desserts.

Chocolate Mendicant Cookies

The toppings represent the four mendicant
traditions united in God. Or the next best thing… chocolate!

Serves 2-3

300 g high cocoa milk chocolate

24 raisins

12 hazelnuts

12 almonds

6 dried figs *sliced*

non-stick baking paper

Boil some water in a pan. Remove from the heat and rest a bowl on top of it so it sits well in the pan but the water doesn't come over the top.

Break the chocolate into the bowl and stir as it starts to melt. Remove the bowl when the chocolate is fully melted, being careful not to get drops of water into the chocolate.

Spread 12 dollops of the melted chocolate onto some baking paper and arrange a hazelnut and almond plus a share of the raisins and fig slices on each.

Allow them to sink into the chocolate.

Leave to cool and peel off the paper when set.

Festive Olive Oil Flatbread

Serves 6

60 g coconut sugar

1 tsp instant yeast

150 ml warm water *approx*

250 g wholemeal bread flour

1 unwaxed orange
grated rind only

1 tbsp extra virgin olive oil

10 ml orange blossom water

pinch of salt

milk *to glaze*

In a jug dissolve the yeast and one tablespoon of the sugar in the warm water. Leave for about 15 minutes for the yeast to activate and become frothy.

Meanwhile mix the flour, salt, orange rind and the rest of the sugar in a bowl. Rub in the oil and orange blossom water. Make a well in the dry ingredients and pour in some of the yeast liquid. Slowly incorporate this into the flour. Mix well and pour in enough of the liquid to form a soft dough that comes away from the sides of the bowl. Add a little more warm water if it is too dry, or flour if it still very sticky.

Knead the dough for about 10 minutes. Place in a large bowl and cover with a tea towel. Leave it to rise in a warm place until it doubles in size—about two hours.

Knead the dough again and form it into a large flat loaf about 1 cm thick. Cut slits into the middle of the bread and place it on a greased tray. Leave it to rise again for about 30 minutes until double in size. Meanwhile, preheat your oven to 200°C. Once the dough has risen, gently brush the top with some milk.

Bake for about 15 minutes until golden and crispy.

Ginger & Orange Cake

Makes 6-8 slices

100 g wholemeal self-raising flour

1 tsp ground ginger

100 g butter

100 g grated jaggery or coconut sugar

1 tbsp maple syrup

1 tbsp grated orange rind

1 tbsp milk or almond milk

2 eggs

Preheat the oven to 175°C.

Grease a 20 cm sandwich cake tin and line the bottom with baking paper.

Blend together the butter, maple syrup and jaggery/coconut sugar with an electric mixer.

Whisk the eggs and milk together in a separate bowl.

Using the mixer, slowly incorporate the eggs and milk into the butter mixture so you get a batter which doesn't separate.

Combine the orange rind, flour and ground ginger in a separate bowl. Stir into the batter and blend well with the mixer until it is light and fluffy.

Pour into the prepared cake tin.

Bake for 20 minutes until firm to the touch.

Cool on a wire tray.

Gateau aux Carottes

Carrots have been used as a natural sweetener in desserts in many
cultures and included in cake recipes since the Middle Ages.

Makes 6-8 slices

2 eggs

100 g grated jaggery or coconut sugar

100 g butter *cut into small pieces*

75 g carrots *peeled & grated*

100g wholemeal self-raising flour

1 tsp mixed spice

25 g desiccated coconut

25 g dates *sliced*

Preheat the oven to 175°C.

Grease a 20 cm sandwich cake tin and line the bottom with baking paper.

Blend together the butter and jaggery/coconut sugar with an electric mixer until creamy.

Whisk the eggs and, using the mixer, slowly incorporate into the butter mixture so they blend together and don't separate.

Add the remaining ingredients and beat well with the cake mixer.

Spoon the mixture into the prepared tin.

Bake for about 20 minutes until the delicious smell fills the kitchen. It should be just firm and golden brown. Remove from the tin and cool on a wire tray.

Crumbling Delight

You may remember cooked school meals as rather unfortunate affairs. But on the days apple crumble was served with its delicious fruit, biscuit topping and lashings of custard, all was forgiven. In the dinner queue we all prayed for crumble… but not tapioca, please!

Serves 4-6

900 g apples *peeled & diced*

100 g blackberries

1 tsp mixed spice

100 g sultanas

50 g grated jaggery or coconut sugar

50 ml water

CRUMBLE TOPPING

250 g kamut or wholemeal flour

125 g butter

60 g coconut sugar

Preheat the oven to 180 °C.

Place the prepared apples, blackberries, jaggery/coconut sugar, sultanas, mixed spice and water in a pan. Bring to the boil and simmer for a few minutes until the apples start to break up.

In a separate bowl, rub the butter into the flour and add the coconut sugar.

Place the apple mix into a 20 cm baking tray.

Cover with the crumble mix.

Bake in the oven for 25–30 minutes.

Serve with hot custard, or fresh cream, sometimes both!

Date Flapjack

Flapjack originally referred to a flat pudding. In the UK it has become synonymous with this oaty biscuit, while in the USA it became a name for pancakes.

Makes 8 slices

250 g butter

125 g maple syrup

125 g grated jaggery or coconut sugar

350 g oats

250 g stoned dates *chopped*

200 ml orange juice

Preheat the oven to 175°C.

Grease a 20 cm baking tray and line it with baking paper.

Heat the dates and orange juice in a pan, simmering until the liquid is absorbed and the dates become mushy.

Meanwhile, in a separate pan, melt the jaggery/coconut sugar, butter and syrup together, then stir in the oats.

Place half the oat mixture into the prepared baking tray and cover with the dates, smoothing them down with the back of a fork. Top with the rest of the oat mix, and smooth down.

Bake for 25–30 minutes, or until golden and cooked through.

Almond Pudding

In this recipe the milk is evaporated, which increases its natural sweetness. The combination of milk, rice and nuts makes this a high protein dish. Rose water is added, not just to make the dish more exotic, but also as a secret love potion! It's thought to help balance the sadhaka pitta, or the 'fire of the heart', which processes our emotions and helps us to give and receive affection. So it's not by chance that roses are the flower of love.

Serves 6–8

1 ltr whole milk

40 g short-grain white rice

¼ tsp ground cardamom

50 g grated jaggery or coconut sugar

60 g almonds

2 tsp rose water *organic if possible*

pinch of ground nutmeg

In a non-stick deep pan combine the milk, rice and cardamom.

Bring to the boil, then simmer over a low heat for about 1 hour, or until it is reduced by about half. Stir occasionally so it doesn't stick or burn.

Remove from the heat and stir in the jaggery/coconut sugar.

Roast and then grind the almonds. Add the almonds and rose water to the pudding.

Serve warm, sprinkled with ground nutmeg.

Chocolate Superfood Cake

Makes 6-8 slices

100 g butter

100 g grated jaggery or coconut sugar

2 eggs

½ tsp almond essence

25 g raw cacao powder

50 g wholemeal self raising flour

25 g ground almonds

2 tbsp chia seeds

Preheat the oven to 175°C.

Grease a 20 cm cake tin and line it with baking paper.

Blend together the butter and jaggery/coconut sugar with an electric mixer until creamy.

Whisk the eggs and, using the mixer, slowly incorporate into the butter mixture so they blend together and don't separate.

Add the remaining ingredients and blend well with the mixer. Spoon the mixture into the prepared tin. Bake in the oven for about 20 minutes, until the delicious smell fills the kitchen. It should be just firm.

Remove from the tin and cool on a wire tray.

Carrot Halva

This is like a creamy vanilla rice custard. In Ayurveda you're not supposed to eat raw fruit with your meals. This dessert recipe gets around that by adding vegetables instead. The carrots make this dish lighter and more nutritious than normal rice pudding.

Serves 6-8

2 tbsp ghee

200 g carrots *peeled & grated*

500 ml whole milk

50 g basmati rice

1 vanilla pod *split lengthways*

50 g grated jaggery or coconut sugar

3 tbsp roasted cashew nuts *chopped*

½ tsp ground cardamom

pinch of ground nutmeg

25 g flaked almonds

Heat the ghee in a non-stick pan. Stir in the carrots and cook for a 2–3 minutes until tender.

Add the milk, rice and vanilla pod.

Simmer for 15 minutes until the rice is soft, stirring regularly so it doesn't stick and burn.

Add the jaggery/coconut sugar.

Stir in the cardamom, nutmeg and cashew nuts and mix well.

Garnish with flaked almonds.

Baked Apples with Date Filling

If you soak almonds overnight they hydrate and start to germinate,
thus activating the enzymes and making them easier to digest. Soaked
almonds are also easier to peel; without the peel they become even more
digestible. Just squeeze one end to pop them out.

Serves 8

200 g almonds *soaked overnight*

25 dried dates *chopped & soaked overnight*

8 dessert apples *cored*

125 ml date syrup

50 g butter

150 ml orange juice

Preheat the oven to 180°C.

Drain the almonds and dates. Peel the almonds, then chop into small pieces and mix with the dates.

Stir in the syrup. Stuff the mixture inside the centre of the cored apples.

Dot the apples with the butter and place them in a baking dish. Pour the orange juice in the bottom of the dish.

Bake for 20–25 minutes, or until the apples are just soft but not collapsed.

Serve warm with some of the cooking juices.

Date & Almond Steamed Pudding

Dates and almonds are highly recommended in Ayurveda.
This recipe is totally gluten-free but as good as any steamed pud.

Serves 8

125 g butter

100 g grated jaggery or coconut sugar

1 egg

1 tsp vanilla extract

200 g ground almonds

2 tbsp desiccated coconut

3 tsp baking powder

¼ tsp salt

½ tsp cinnamon

½ tsp ground cardamom

1 tsp ground ginger

120 ml milk

100 g dates *chopped*

Cream the butter and the jaggery/coconut sugar together (you may need to warm the jaggery slightly to make it soft). Add the egg and beat until well mixed.

Stir in the vanilla extract and beat again.

In a separate bowl, mix together the ground almonds, coconut, salt, baking powder and spices, then fold into the butter mixture in stages, alternating with the milk. Keep stirring until everything is mixed well, then add the dates.

Pour into a buttered mould or small bowl (about 15 cm diameter). Seal well using a sheet each of baking paper and foil (with the foil on top of the paper) and tying them around the bowl with string.

Steam for 2 hours. Serve with custard or cream.

Rice Pudding

Rice pudding originated in Asia, but it soon caught on in the West as rice, sugar and spices were traded around the world. Now nearly every country has a version of this delicious pudding. In the UK it is sold in tins as 'Ambrosia Cream Pudding', which is aptly named—a food fit for the gods.

Serves 4

60 g short grain white rice

600 ml whole milk

2 tbsp grated jaggery or coconut sugar

1 thin strip lemon rind

15 g butter *cut into small pieces*

ground nutmeg *to taste*

¼ tsp cinnamon

Preheat the oven to 150°C.

Wash the rice and drain in a sieve.

Put it into an ovenproof dish.

In a bowl, mix together the milk, jaggery/coconut sugar and lemon rind. Add to the rice.

Sprinkle the nutmeg and cinnamon over the top.

Dot with the butter pieces.

Place in the oven and bake for about 2 hours, or until the pudding has a golden-brown skin and the rice is tender and creamy but not dried out.

Index & Appendix

INDEX OF INGREDIENTS

INDEX OF RECIPES

Spice Mixes

Sundries

Vegetables Sides

MY BLOG

So you've finished reading this book and perhaps you're not wanting your enjoyment to end? You may even be feeling a tiny bit jealous of other people who haven't read it yet and still have that pleasure to come? Or if they're still on the first few pages, you might be tempted to tell them the best bits?

We hope 'Cooking with Love' has been like a good meal—nourishing and enjoyable. Just to keep you topped up, there are some free snacks available on my blog 'Keith on Food'. Any time you feel like a new morsel of information, you can simply go online.

'Keith on Food' has regular posts on nutrition and detox, as well as recipes and stories I've picked up from my travels. It's totally free and available 24/7 on your computer. Plus, it has a friendly format for your tablet, phone or even a smartwatch. You can have different pages open on separate devices if you want. As there are regular updates with exciting new information, you can even use it as your screensaver so you don't miss any new posts.

Go to **keithonfood.com** for:

> natural detox techniques

> Ayurveda tips

> yoga and meditation

> recipes and nutrition

> stories and inspiration

> lots of pictures.

keithonfood.com

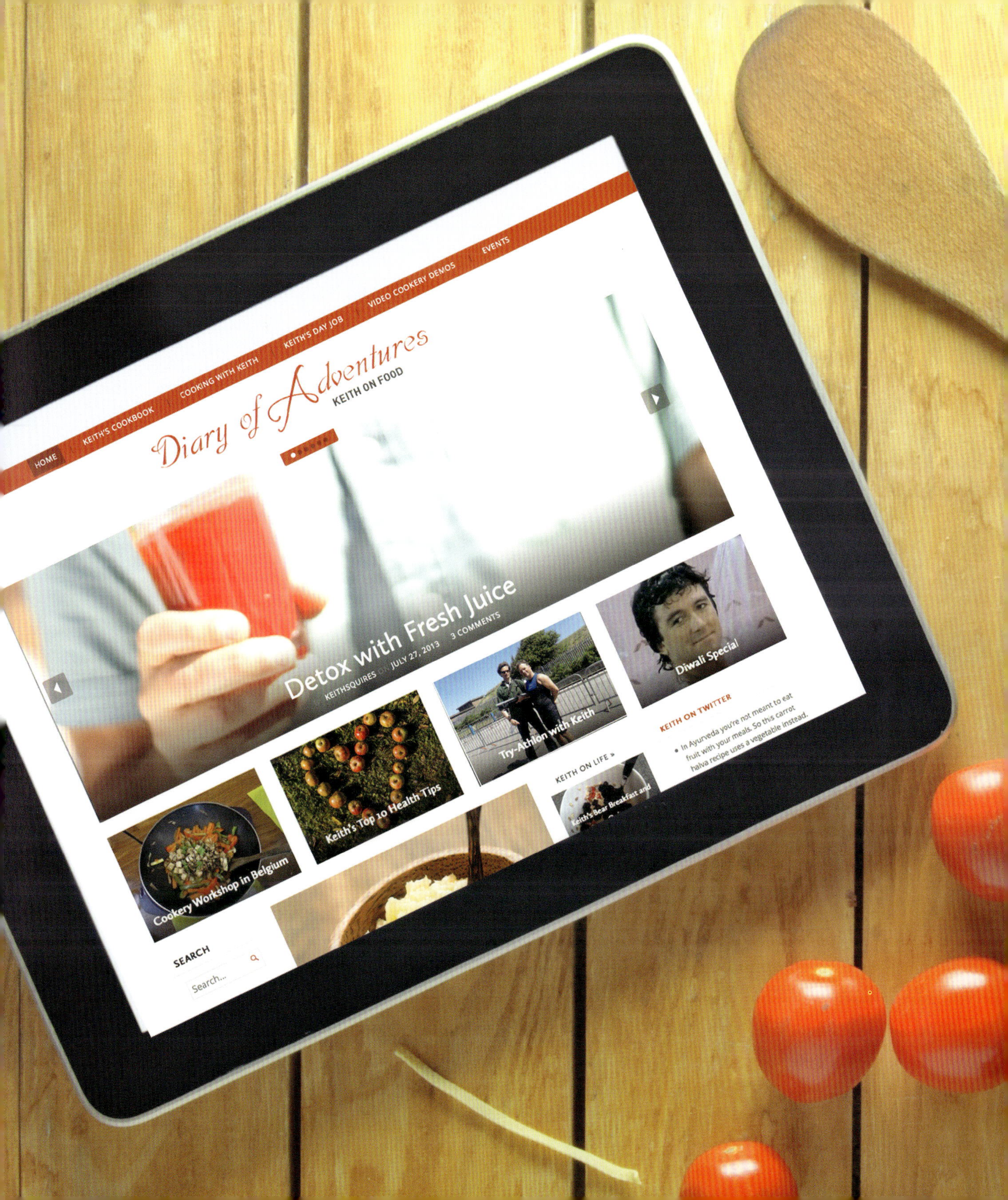

EVENTS
VIDEO COOKERY DEMOS
KEITH'S DAY JOB
COOKING WITH KEITH
KEITH'S COOKBOOK
HOME
Diary of Adventures
KEITH ON FOOD
Detox with Fresh Juice
KEITHSQUIRES ON JULY 27, 2013   3 COMMENTS
Diwali Special
Try-Athlon with Keith
Keith's Top 10 Health Tips
KEITH ON LIFE »
Keith's Bear Breakfast and
Cookery Workshop in Belgium
KEITH ON TWITTER
In Ayurveda you're not meant to eat
fruit with your meals. So this carrot
halva recipe uses a vegetable instead.
SEARCH
Search...

KEITH ON AYURVEDA—eBOOK

If you have enjoyed reading about Ayurveda and would like to know more, my ebook is the perfect follow-on. For the price of a good cup of coffee, you can start practising real Ayurveda straight away. There's a lot more detail about the constitution types, understanding the six tastes and making Ayurveda part of your daily routine. I explain the techniques and philosophy in an easy-to-understand, fun and practical way. There are some totally new Ayurvedic recipes, including the South Indian 'dosa'. This is a crispy rice pancake with a delicious filling, spicy sauce and coconut chutney. Now you can have a dosa for your dosha!

In Ayurveda they say the biggest obstacle to your health is procrastination. We put things off (good food, exercise or yoga) always planning to start tomorrow. But disease doesn't wait—it slowly and invisibly gets established. It spreads its tentacles, waiting for the perfect time to appear. 'Keith on Ayurveda' is like a manual to help you untangle these roots of disease and banish them from your body. Allow your health to rule supreme!

Inside the ebook:

> how to understand your dosha

> Ayurvedic cooking and the six tastes

> Ayurvedic living in the modern world

> dinacharya: your daily detox routine

> Ayurvedic recipes and home remedies.

keithonfood.com/ebooks

Thank you to my
wonderful wife,
Samia, who edited
and designed
this book

ACKNOWLEDGMENTS

First of all I would like to thank my parents, Kevin and Marjory, whose kindness and encouragement made my journey with cooking possible. From mud pies in the garden and childhood recipes written out in crayon, to this cookbook today, thank you for always supporting my dreams.

I am eternally grateful to my wife, Samia, who produced, edited and designed this book. Like you, it is a thing of beauty.

Much gratitude to everyone who I've worked with over the years at Dru. You have been the inspiration behind this book. A project like this is a team effort, with hours of hidden work behind the scenes.

Thank you Kate Couldwell, for your experienced proofreading and for your kindness and generous support.

 A special mention also goes to Suzanne Galloway, our expert photographer; your fantastic skills have inspired this book's 'look and feel'.

Thanks to May Ritchie and Rika Lukac for swooping in at the eleventh hour with your eagle eyes.

Mouli Mackenzie, thank you for your immense help with the pre-press process; without you it would have been extremely difficult to get everything right for the printer.

I'd like to wholeheartedly thank my magnificent proofreaders: Graham Burgess, Merry Pearson, Nigel Morrison, Hilary Airey, Anne Smale and Hilary Bichovsky for all the love, time and effort you put into this project.

An enormous acknowledgement must go to the Dru Centre cooks, past and present, who have poured their own creativity and love into producing varied, delicious and healthy meals over the years.

Last but not least, I'd like to thank myself. It all took a lot longer than I first expected but I stuck at it, sacrificing an amazing trip to Kenya last year. Even my laptop gave up under the pressure—a treasured Christmas gift whose little lights faded for the last time in September 2015.

Thanks again to all of you for your efforts, your support and your help in coming up with a result that we can be proud of.

ABOUT DRU

We are an energetic and fresh-thinking, not-for-profit social enterprise founded on the ideal of giving back to the world.

Our birth as a company was almost 40 years ago when a small group of idealistic university students sought to transform the world by giving people the tools to transform themselves.

Since the beginning, the major passion we all shared was our love for yoga and meditation. It was through these practices that we initially wanted to help people find a healthier and more empowered way of living. Of course, we recognise these are only two of the many routes to achieving a more fulfilling existence.

Since then, Dru has grown into an international School of Yoga, Meditation, Ayurveda, Health and Nutrition, with training centres located throughout the UK, The Netherlands and Australia. Our passion is to create educational programmes for positive health and wellbeing in order to inspire a natural and healthier way of living for everybody.

druyoga.com

DRU YOGA

For more than 30 years, we've been teaching Dru Yoga worldwide to people of all ages, fitness levels, walks of life, abilities—and even disabilities! Dru is now one of the largest yoga organisations. We've trained thousands of yoga teachers, meditation teachers and yoga therapists. From war zones to workplaces everywhere, Dru has been tried and tested in many settings. It's underpinned by scientific research showing its extensive health benefits. (Hartfiel et al, 2011, 2012, 2014, 2017).

Scientific research shows that Dru Yoga:

- ✓ increases energy levels
- ✓ maintains a healthy back
- ✓ improves resilience to stress
- ✓ enhances emotional wellbeing
- ✓ reduces susceptibility to injuries.

As a result, Dru Yoga is now being integrated into schools, hospitals, government agencies, large and small businesses, professional sports and in nearly every sector of society.

Visit **druyogaonline.com** to explore hundreds of online classes in the comfort of your own home. New videos are uploaded regularly on nutrition, yoga, yoga dance, yoga therapy, meditation, ayurveda, vedic astrology, kirtan, vegetarian cookery, health tips and much much more.

druyogaonline.com

A study published in September 2012 in the Journal of Occupational Medicine, showed that Dru Yoga significantly reduced both stress and back pain at work—two of the key factors leading to sickness absence at work. After an eight-week programme, the Dru Yoga group scores (when compared with the Control group) were significantly lower for perceived stress, back pain, sadness and hostility, and significantly higher for feeling self-assured, attentive and serene.

A 2016 study sponsored by Bangor University and the NHS found that an eight-week Dru Yoga programme resulted in less back pain, fewer sickness absence days, and cost-saving for the NHS. See graphs.

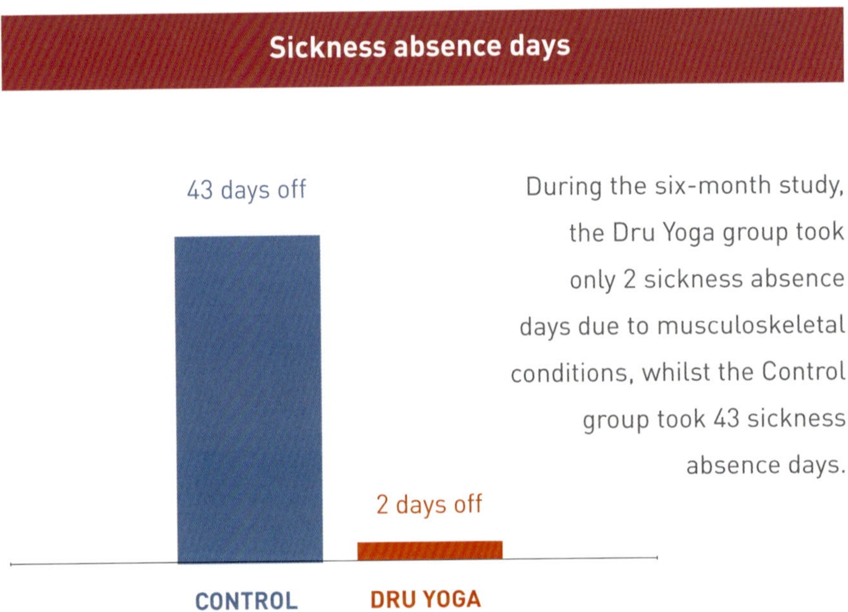

During the six-month study, the Dru Yoga group took only 2 sickness absence days due to musculoskeletal conditions, whilst the Control group took 43 sickness absence days.

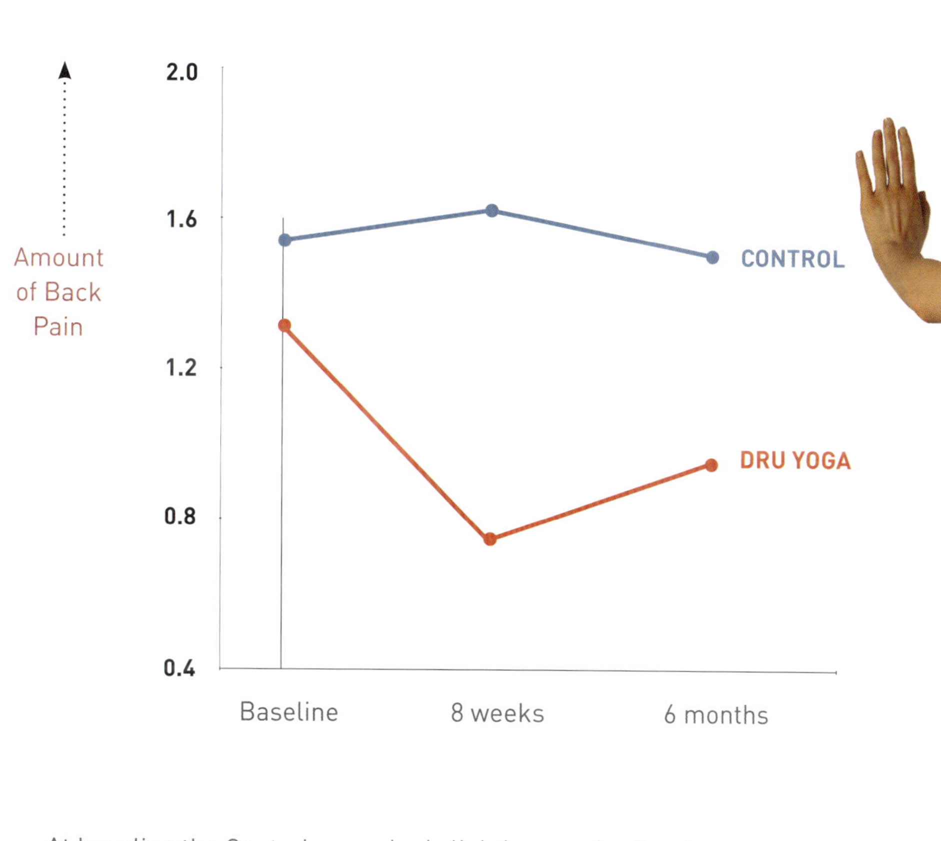

At baseline the Control group had slightly more back pain than the Dru Yoga group.

After the eight-week programme, the Dru Yoga group had significantly less back pain.

At the six-month follow-up, the Dru Yoga group still had less back pain, even without the weekly classes.

Four Thieves
Vinegar
page 173

FOOD PHOTOGRAPHY

Suzanne Galloway

Samia Squires

References

Harfiel, N., Edwards, R.T. and Phillips, C. (2014) The Cost-Effectiveness of Yoga for Preventing and Reducing Back Pain at Work: Trial Protocol. *Journal of Yoga and Physical Therapy*, 4:161.

Hartfiel, N., Burton, C., Rycroft-Malone, J., Clarke, G., Havenhand, J., Khalsa, S.B. and Edwards, R.T. (2012). Yoga for reducing perceived stress and back pain at work. *Occupational Medicine*, (62)8: 606-612.

Hartfiel, N., Havenhand, J., Khalsa, S.B., Clarke, G. and Krayer, A. (2011). The effectiveness of yoga for the improvement of wellbeing and resilience to stress in the workplace. *Scandinavian Journal of Work, Environment and Health*, 37(1):70-76.

Vegetarian diets in the Adventist Health Study 2: a review of initial published findings. Orlich, Michael J; Fraser, Gary E. *The American Journal of Clinical Nutrition.* 2014 Jun; 100(Supplement 1):353S-358S

Stock photos

© Istockphoto.com/vladmax, swkunst, squaredpixels, dirk rietschel, mashuk, dulezidar, bobbie osborne, alleko, duron123, elizabeth shoemaker, boyarkinamarina, philipimage, nick white, fotoedu, zkruger, jack_pierce, ockra, zakharova_natalia, spanishalex, lepas2004, pleasureofart, klenova, elena schweitzer, elena sychugina, dumitru doru, lise gagne, lise gagne, olga forster, bradleym, beng beng tan, szymon mazurek, jã¶rg jahn, appleuzr, dragan trifunovic, andrzej burak, sxn, dirk diesel, ene, mediaphotos, imaginegolf © Adobestock.com/tan4ikk, mara zemgaliete, pixelbliss, sahilu11, shersor, nitr, saratm

Published in the United Kingdom 2017

Dru Publications, Dru (UK), Nant Ffrancon, Bethesda
Bangor, North Wales LL57 3LX
+44 (0)1248 602900 | hello@druworldwide.com | druyoga.com

Published in Australia 2017

40 MacFarland Crescent, Chifley, ACT 2607

ISBN 978-1-873606-38-4
A CIP catalogue record for this book is available from the British Library.

Author Keith Squires

Editor Samia Squires

Book and cover design Samia Squires
Cover photographs Suzanne Galloway

Photography Suzanne Galloway, Samia Squires, Mouli Mackenzie
Tim Hollis, Ffion Hughes, John Versfeld

Pre-press support Mouli MacKenzie

Printed in China by Everbest Printing